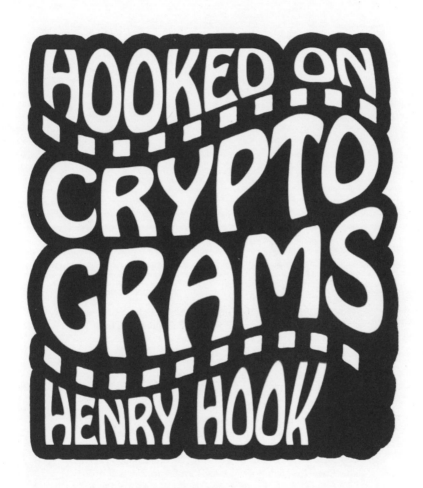

# HOOKED ON CRYPTO GRAMS

## HENRY HOOK

**PUZZLE WRIGHT PRESS**

An imprint of Sterling
Publishing Co., Inc.

**www.puzzlewright.com**

Puzzlewright Press and the distinctive Puzzlewright Press logo are
registered trademarks of Sterling Publishing Co., Inc.

4  6  8  10  9  7  5

Published by Sterling Publishing Co., Inc.
387 Park Avenue South, New York, NY 10016
© 2010 by Henry Hook
Distributed in Canada by Sterling Publishing
C/o Canadian Manda Group, 165 Dufferin Street
Toronto, Ontario, Canada M6K 3H6
Distributed in the United Kingdom by GMC Distribution Services
Castle Place, 166 High Street, Lewes, East Sussex, England BN7 1XU
Distributed in Australia by Capricorn Link (Australia) Pty. Ltd.
P.O. Box 704, Windsor, NSW 2756, Australia

*Printed in China*

Sterling ISBN 978-1-4027-7457-7

For information about custom editions, special sales, premium and
corporate purchases, please contact Sterling Special Sales
Department at 800-805-5489 or specialsales@sterlingpublishing.com.

# CONTENTS

# INTRODUCTION

Thumbing through these pages, one might think someone overturned a huge vat of alphabet soup. But you, my esteemed solvers, know of course that each serving of noodle jumble is really a sentence in disguise. Most of these sentences are humorous quotations spoken by some rather funny folks; a few others are my own somewhat misguided attempts at humor; and once in a while you'll disclose an interesting bit of odd trivia. You should be warned that I have a twisted, some might even say sick, sense of humor. I tried in this book to offend everyone equally.

Those of you familiar with my past work, primarily crosswords, may wonder why I opted to compose a book of cryptograms. Two reasons: 1) Every so often, a person needs something different; 2) The New York State Lottery Commission still steadfastly refuses to draw my numbers. (I only have to sell about a half-billion copies of this book to match the current jackpot.)

If you find yourself stuck on a puzzle, you may turn to page 159 for an initial hint. A second hint may be found on the following page.

Enjoy.

—Henry Hook

**1**

FUN THING TO DO ON A REALLY

KYZ HQLZX HM GM MZ I NOICCS

DULL SUNDAY AFTERNOON. TRY

GYCC FYZGIS IKHONZMMZ: HNS

SOLVING THE NEW YORK TIMES

FMCALZX HQO ZOJ SMND HLEOF

CROSSWORD USING ONLY PIECES

TNMFFJMNG YFLZX MZCS ULOTOF

OF MAGNETIC POETRY

MK "EIXZOHLT UMOHNS."


**2**

MESSAGE FROM A RECENT

DURRPJU HBND P BUQUOG

FORTUNE COOKIE    NO ONE IS

HNBGMOU QNNTVU: "ON NOU VR

EVER TOO OLD TO LEARN BUT

UCUB GNN NSW GN SUPBO, YMG

MANY PEOPLE KEEP PUTTING IT

DPOI LUNLSU TUUL LMGGVOJ VG

OFF ANYWAY

NHH POIZPI."


**3**

ALWAYS FORGIVE YOUR

HVUHJE RMOIQLZ JMBO

ENEMIES NOTHING ANNOYS

ZFZDQZE; FMGKQFI HFFMJE

THEM SO MUCH

GKZD EM DBYK.

OSCAR WILDE

—MEYHO UQVXZ


**4**

IT'S AMAZING HOW MUCH WORK

NX'F WBWUNGJ PQH BLVP HQMD

I COULD HAVE DONE IN THE

N VQLCO PWIZ OQGZ NG XPZ

TIME I'VE SPENT WAITING FOR

XNBZ N'IZ FSZGX HWNXNGJ AQM

MY COMPUTER TO START

BR VQBSLXZM XQ FXWMX.

**5**

PHYSICIAN SOMEONE TO
XKPBMYMIQ: BTZNTQN AT

WHOM YOU GIVE EXORBITANT
RKTZ PTV DMFN NCTELMAIQA

AMOUNTS OF MONEY TO TELL
IZTVQAB TH ZTQNP AT ANWW

YOU THINGS YOU WERE HAPPIER
PTV AKMQDB PTV RNEN KIXXMNE

NOT KNOWING
QTA SQTRMQD.


**6**

ORGANIZED CRIME IN AMERICA
BNXDHFGOY PNFKO FH DKONFPD

TAKES IN OVER FORTY MILLION
UDQOV FH BION SBNUE WFCCFBH

DOLLARS A YEAR AND SPENDS
YBCCDNV D EODN DHY VJOHYV

VERY LITTLE ON OFFICE
IONE CFUUCO BH BSSFPO

SUPPLIES
VRJJCFOV.

WOODY ALLEN
—ZBBYE DCCOH


**7**

YOU KNOW THERE IS A PROBLEM
JQX ZHQF WYPLP SG T KLQUMPC

C=M

WITH THE EDUCATION SYSTEM
FSWY WYP PVXETWSQH GJGWPC

WHEN YOU REALIZE THAT OUT
FYPH JQX LPTMSAP WYTW QXW

OF THE THREE R'S ONLY ONE
QN WYP WYLPP L'G, QHMJ QHP

BEGINS WITH R
UPOSHG FSWY L.

DENNIS MILLER
—VPHHSG CSMMPL

**8**

IT TOOK ME SEVENTEEN YEARS

RJ JNNP LS DSFSIJSSI BSWAD

TO GET THREE THOUSAND HITS

JN USJ JYASS JYNVDWIG YRJD

IN BASEBALL. I DID IT IN

RI ZWDSZWXX. R GRG RJ RI

ONE AFTERNOON ON THE GOLF

NIS WMJSAINNI NI JYS UNXM

COURSE

QNVADS.

HANK AARON

—YWIP WWANI

**9**

I HAVE LOW SELF ESTEEM WHEN

P RTHV ZWI EVZQ-VEXVVS. IRVC

WE WERE IN BED TOGETHER I

IV IVOV PC JVK XWAVXRVO, P

WOULD FANTASIZE THAT I WAS

IWDZK QTCXTEPUV XRTX P ITE

SOMEONE ELSE

EWSVWCV VZEV.

RICHARD LEWIS

—OPFRTOK ZVIPE

**10**

WE'RE                    VE EVERY   Y

TU'KU GIWL GI WZAU UAUKB LFB

            WERE      R

FD ZP ZG TUKU IMK WFDG. DI

    Y        E            E

GILFB Z OFAU FX FRRIZXGYUXG

  E              E

GI VU FMGIRDZUL.

**11** HOYRO MSO TPTOVM. JOTOTGOJ

ECC MSPHO FPTOV PV MSO

MYMEVYB FSP FENOW PXX MSO

WOHHOJM BEJM.

—OJTE GPTGOBZ


**12** P LGFQ IE YCEVXPHLBPCL LXHL

KSKBEGJK XHLKC IK. XK CHPQ

P RHC WKPJD BPQPVZFGZC;

KSKBEGJK XHCJ'L IKL IK EKL.

—BGQJKE QHJDKBMPKFQ


**13** Y CVP JXRNK HVAVYBJ R.J.

JXRNVCXJ LYAV AVHK BWXXBV

FCSPBVNIV SG YEVHWZYC

LWJXSHK. WC GYZX, XVJX JZSHVJ

YHV XLV BSPVJX JWCZV XLV

BWCZSBC-CWDSC NVOYXVJ.

—ZSCYC S'OHWVC

**14** LG OJB EOJZWRY.... TIIRYTJEC TB LOR SRC. DTLO RGRPCQZR LDTLLRPTZW ZQD, TZKQPIJLTQZ TB QZUC WQQY KQP JVQHL J YJC.

—FJC URZQ

**15** KQB YZO ZG DW DPDXZWO DWZPDH. ZL RCM LBBT D YZO DW DYYHB, ZK PDEBG SDICW. Z LZWT KQDK ZPYJBGGZUB.

—VZP ODLLZODW

**16** OQGZG'T TF JCIQ HBKTODI DP OQDT ICBOCZG OQKO ADPNB BGFHKZW TLDP DT UGIFJDPM KP GPWKPMGZGW TNPOQGODI.

—BDBN OFJBDP

**17**  D GHHUJIHSO XJ HYO HL INO
HYEM RXOTOJ HL OKXPOYTO AO
NDKO INDI ROHREO DSO JIXEE
INXYUXYZ.

—VOSSM JOXYLOEP

**18**  OI'A OXETCIQDI IT CNXNXUNC
IRQI QEEQCNDIJK, UK
NJOXODQIOTD, ZOARTDNAIK OA
IRN ANYTDZ-UNAI ETJOYK.

—SNTCSN YQCJOD

**19**  S ONM'B HSGX BJX SOXT BJTB
KXNKHX ETM ETHH ZNV SM
ZNVW ETW. S BJSMG BJXWX'D
MXFD ZNV DJNVHOM'B YXB TB
DSLBZ PSHXD TM JNVW.

—BNP KTWGD

**20** KUU CPXHX CN DXKUJCL HPZVH
SKEX SX VZFMXD ... JH CPXDX
KFLZFX, KFLVPXDX, VPZS
KQHZUGCXUL FZQZML CPJFEH
FXXMH K SKEXZNXD?

**21** DTPIRYQ IPYJTZ YQ JMPQTM KM
QMI ORCT R AMPK BMP "QM"
RQK DMQZTGWTQIXN IWPQ
KMAQ PTGWTZIZ JN QMKKYQF
IOTYP OTRKZ RQK ZRNYQF "Y'XX
FTI JRDU IM NMW."

—AMMKN RXXTQ

**22** LKFF GV XM LKJQEGSO VOKVQH
GH FQV KHNOFOV, CKSBPGHN
SPO ZGEYV BPKHNO BQFQE KHY
LKFF LEQX SPO SEOOV.

—YKJGY FOSSOEXKH

**23** CSUGU BGU OBCGYACYM
NUWUCBGYBLZ YL CSU
BJUGYMBL TUWYAL ESA EYTT
ALTI UBC BLYJBTZ CSBC EUGU
DYTTUK YL MAJVBC.

—WUAGWU MBGTYL

**24** EN AFQ WENFOLJR DJ PN ALOE
ELQ QNWXNOFXU. L BDYJT
GLIQOLWZ DJ ELQ WDGGFX,
WDCNXNT ALOE ALON-DYO.

—ANJTU GLNSPFJ

**25** BCOHO MYX YW JBOU JW BCO
EYEOH BQFYI: Y SJQW KQB
SQQXO JW BCO TOWBHYS EYHN
AQQ JW WOM IQHN, YWF MYX
XOGOHOSI UYRSOF.

—PQP WOMCYHB

**26** XPJJTPIK TA JKPC DZOIM
WKRPOAK EZO MPHK DZ YKPC
GTDM NKKCTQIA, PQY CPGEKJA.

—JTRMPJY LJEZJ

**27** E SXBZYO ZM WHG X DXBOTY
PMTOYV WHZ ZPY RZMVY OEOB'Z
PXQY MBY, RM E UMZ X DXNY.

—IEZDP PYOWYVU

**28** U QZUHP HUL HDKOOSBT XKND
EULJ OSTBSWSYO LJUL LJY
UBSAUZ SO TKSBT OKAYIJYDY.

—TDKNHJK AUDG

**29** RPPTSWO OZG VNSDQG XZYQ
QYQNHPWQ GLAWWQJ.... VQPVMQ
SW M.Z. TZH GQNSPAGMH GLZNL
LXSWISWO ZUPAL FZMISWO LXQ
LFP UMPDIG LP LXQ GLPNQ.

—BZH MQWP

**30**  YFWWM UET YN BDPRQNS
BDEV JEBNS, YIB PB PA ABPFF
ABPRQT, IVKFNEAEVB, EVM
LNVNSEFFT VEIANEBPVL

—XEVNEVN LESWOEFW

**31**  QMM SAY COKIMYTW FY XQEY ZJ
SAY PJZSYL WSQSYW SKLQB EQJ
IY SOQEYL SK QJ PJYJMZRASYJYL
ZTTZROQSZKJ CKMZEB KJ SAY
CQOS KX SAY QTYOZEQJ ZJLZQJ.

—CQS CQPMWYJ

**32**  AXIRZTZKGB KU TB KPMX TBP
VGUZ STMUX KVIGUKZKGB, GSZ
NGZ OKZWGRZ VXAKZ TBP MGUZ
OKZWGRZ PXUXADKBN.

—OKMMKTV UWTYXUIXTAX

15

**33**  SLTDT'F BTNMST URA RU
ALTSLTD HXKRSF FLROKB IMDDQ
EOUF. RU SLT RUT LMUB, SLT
FWXTF AROKB NT FMVTD. RU
SLT RSLTD LMUB, EOUF MUB
MKIRLRK BRU'S PXG.

— IRUMU R'NDXTU

**34**  O ZHM'U KRNKLU IMBHMK UH
IAQKK JOUP IWW TB DHUKG.
O ZHM'U IAQKK JOUP IWW HE
UPKT TBGKWE.

— IQWKM GNKLUKQ

**35**  B FMJJTVW GDD TK B WSMBJ
FRBNM, TZ HDX QBVJ HDXS
LTP'K NRDJCMK JD MVP XF
TVKTPM B WDBJ'K KJDABNC.

— ETR PQHMS

**36** CTW XWHYXI AYX TPQTWLC-
LHYXPEQ LPEQMW FMKV PE K
LHXKUUMW QKGW PL CTXWW
TNEIXWI LPZCV-APJW FYPECL.
CTW BYXI BKL "ONPZYCXV."

**37** JR YACZ TI T QRX'Z ACBO "CWJ
RI JZOOF"? TJX'Z TZ DRRQ
OXRVDA ZACZ T ACBO C KCJZ-
TLRX JZRNCKA?

**38** YRLT OEQ'BL NT CEFL, NA'W ARL
KEWA ZCEBNEQW AYE JTM J RJCP
MJOW EP OEQB CNPL.

                        —BNGRJBM CLYNW

**39** EO ES'L SMG RLUVMEV
HGSQPYB, QMU XP SMGU HGGX
D RMPHG HJAZGY?

                        —YPZEH QENNEDAL

**40** NUVDSUQ WVTZUDA ATVQU HU.
DSCMZ VOXYD CD, EUXENU VQU
... AEUMICML RCGU SYMIQUI
IXNNVQA DX PUVQ OUUR
WUQZK.

—OQVI ADCMU

**41** KCYYBWI EVUE EVW DVYULW
SBXVE QW YWSCZWI NYCS O.L.
SCAWR, U GVBGUXC LGVCCP
QOL IYBZWY DWEBEBCAWI EC
PWXUPPR GVUAXW VBL AUSW EC
"BA XCI KW EYOLE."

**42** VXAYH YJ RVEYFRVH XFCEAM
QFREO ... IOYZO YJ JYHHM,
LCZVGJC RFEOYRU AOMQCJ
IYEO "VXAYH" FA "QFREO."
JOFGHKR'E YE LC V KVM YR
QVM? FA V DGRC VSECARFFR?

**43** WJNWOJ HQN PNS'X JFX JSNKBQ
ZFTMY DCBQX MJ YLCSSV, MKX
FTJS'X XQJV FOHFVY ZTFSLV?

—TFZQFJO TFV

**44** VUBAM ZXM OMUGZX WLM
SJOOMXW CYOGW CUVYPB
XUVMT WLMYO FJFFB AZ YG
WLUW "ZAUVU AZ" YG U
FUPYXTOZVM? XUL, FOZAUAPB
XZW.

**45** JU'K UCXD: V ZESVB QCES
BECQEOI, DBWOVBL, CDADBUOH
ODVCBDL KFD FVL RDDB
ADODRCVUJBW FDC RJCUFLVH
EBD LVH OVUD QEC EPDC V
ADBUXCH.

**46** WEJID VW JG RGEJQQH DISCVSG
VGBDGCDZ AH QVDCVWCW VG
SNZDN CS DPQFSVC CED ERIJG
NJOD.

—KNSI CED WONDDGQFJH
"BVOCSN/BVOCSNVJ"

**47** NGQW DA UKJ LUJK JGVMJQJLKU.
RDAJ JGNN DA ZCGYG LJ LA;
ZG'NN BLUW LJ.

—AQV NGPGUAKU

**48** G DBZFI CHMVKT GF FBISGFX
VKMV MB SYAAH / YM GF Y
MBZK UVCVCPVUGFX CH XBBJ
TUGVFJM.

—LGKKGYC MSYOVMAVYUV
"UGDSYUJ GG"

**49** UAN INHMNU UR PQJTOL TI
UR UAMRY JRVMINQP WU UAN
LMRVOK WOK CTII.

—PMRC "UAN ATUHAATSNM'I
LVTKN UR UAN LWQWFJ"

**50** ATZAG VBYYKX, RLCSBKQKQW
TFI RBXE KM IBX MF AYRBMR
"QRISEIRO WBPR": "BSS K
QRRORO IBX UFZY AFZCSRX,
RKWTM DZRXMKFQX, BQO B
IBXTRY-OYERY."

**51** HOW ZWHPRQ YKYHWZ TRT GXH
PWBIIK QBHQO XG RG HOW
YHBHWY, AGIWYY KXA QXAGH
HOW RGQPWBYRGC DXDAIBPRHK
XJ HOW GRGW-ZRIIRZWHWP
MAIIWH.

—TBUW MBPPK

**52**  NAYL ZF NUTY XMDYK ZY QS
MQXPQ X IXPKYL, QAY TUPMQ
QAULI U KGI GW NXM XL
YJBGMY.

—AYLLF FSGLIZXL

**53**  BI WTX CWIROVPDX GFPX HW
FZI, "V OPZX STZICWI RWO HAP
ZOHVLTPF." OVNAH, ZDX V NW
HW FAWSSVDN BZTTF RWO HAP
BGFVL.

—OVHZ OGXDPO

**54**  QNN IJSE: TQRYAYJ WJG J
BJAJR IQMSF DYEW EWQHGJBNG
QI GJYRQMG JBN QAFM QBF
WHBNMFN IYIEC TQJEG, NFGUYEF
TFYBO J RJBNRQSPFN BJEYQB.

**55** S EFSTK GSF WVSZXK QZXV

S VSMQV UKSHX NTWDQRW

GRWWTFO TWEXKI. QV WQ JRW

TW SFQWDXV NSB, EGTXFWTEWE

OXW UQVXH.

—LTYYB GSVV


**56** CZK LZOF JP DVF WOK MVC UVG.

DVR, WSGZ-YCZZD LZOF ...

FIOF'P WOK MVC UVG.

—FVLLU PLVFIZCP


**57** S HXZANSH DAFMWBXH SM BL

NWDSN VQKXH DWBTNSQKXV

UJXK MJX THQDXF UXKM AT. Q

MWNV JQB QM USF IXDSAFX

MJXL JSV MW WRRFXM MJX

DWFM WR THQKMQKZ BXKAF

UQMJ MJX KXU THQDXF WK

MJXB.

**58** NUAABUYL BO WBSL U ZBFL-
KQCDOUMT-RBLXL IBYOUP
RDVVWL, UWW OSG.

—XUKQG WUTNUM

**59** NYMWNA-FMC TWMFSILWF
LFDZTLJ PWSK Z UZME MI NYL
ZPWMDZI IZNMSI SP RHMILZ GA
JMRRMIR NYWSHRY Z VZEE VMNY
FTSSIF.

**60** R NOPC TCPCY UODHNCW
"OACYRHOT RWIQ," GFD R'A
DNOTVBFQ UC'YC QRPRTK RT
O HIFTDYL UNCYC UC HOT
OHDFOQQL OBBIYW DI UOMDC
LIFY DRAC.

—OYQI KFDNYRC

**61**  ZD FGM LXQI ZC X DWYAPU

LZFFUM PF OXWO "SXW QXAOM

BJZROPDMOO." PF OGZAUB OXW

"BZD'F SXIM XDW TUXDO."

—BMDPO UMXJW

**62**  VGRCGT YVG ST V ZCUD

VGGCFGYTI. VUU RCF BVHT EC

OC NX FXT EBVE HCNYT RCF FXT

MBTG RCF YVUU NG XNYL VE

MCIL.

—QNLT ICMT

**63**  EUQTUOT QKYIX XTJJ AUH XIRX

QRCCKRYT KE PHEX R BKTFT UM

BRBTC. DTJJ, EU KE QUOTA, ROZ

DIRX'E QUCT JKMT-RMMKCQKOY

XIRO FUJZ, IRCZ FREI?

—ZTOOKE QKJJTC

**64**  BOBA GRWMB WRWBVBBW-
VEBWVF-WRWB, VTB MRVRXBWG
KQ NDAURWJVKW, ERGMKWGRW,
TPOB TBUS PW PWWDPU
MKWVBGV VK SBVBAZRWB ETK
VTBRA NRJJBGV URPA RG.

**65**  BGDGNDQS QB JFCNC LFC
XCOCZRHCN DGZZXRPCB RGL
LFC LNCCB, LFCT TSVCB LFC
BLNCCLB SILCN LFCV.

                    —DQZZ OSGUFST

**66**  "YIJIMVIFEK" EL ZQCEDQZ KL
"K CQKN IC UINZL." FPA EC SIP
VKRQ K CQKN IC UINZL, VIU ZI
SIP AQYY AVQ MLSXVEKANELA?
AVQ TITQDA VQ KLHL "UVKA'L
AVQ MNIFYQT?" SIP'YY NPD
LXNQKTEDJ!

**67** GI G HFU ZFGW F WEQQFN IEN
LMLNV YGKL KV WFW UFGW DL
QEMLW KL.... HLQQ, KEXLV
GUX'Y GKZENYFXY XEH.

—QFNNV YDL OFRQL SJV

**68** ZSH MCNHE D PHZ, ZSH
TDGOCHE ZSH NHVDRDZDMR
MV GBZXEDZJ THHGT: DZ'T ZSH
CHRPZS MV ZDGH FHZQHHR
QSHR D EHBCDKH TMGHMRH DT
B LBAYBTT BRN QSHR D ZHCC
ZSHG ZSBZ ZSHJ'EH MRH.

—FEHZZ FXZCHE

**69** SZO SOPZBQXQLMPWX WICWBPO
M RMJZ M PQTXI LOS MJ WB
WIIMSMQB SQ YK WBJROAMBL
YWPZMBO: W LOS-SQ-SZO-
EQMBS HTSSQB.

—WXMPMW HAWBIS

27

**70** GUFYF RM ZE RIFW ME
AWGFZGPC WLMOYI GUWG RG
KWZ'G KWGKU EZ.

—LRPP TWUFY

**71** IGENBCG FB ZGI QBXJ, IDGXG
GTGXQ FBRXUYF UY P IPEJUZM
PFC CPNDUZG.

—OPTUO EGFFGXCPZ

**72** R YBRCF R HW H NAIYYJ QDDV
UOVQI DE NIDNXI, TBRZB RG TBJ
R BHYI WDGY DE YBIW.

—ADGIHCCI SHAA

**73** A'JB XATTBZ UI YDOH CTDOFU. A
KDTXBZ AOFI D OSLUBLH IOMB,
DOZ YH GDMB KDU IO D KDOFBZ
CIUFBL.

—LAFD LSZOBL

**74**   W TBV DGPGQBC
BPGUZTGUWB.... KRF DR ZR
UCGGY WP RPG QRRN, BPV ZTGP
IBOG FY JRFQ TRFQU CBZGQ WP
B ZRZBCCK VWJJGQGPZ QRRN.
HFUZ CWOG MRCCGDG.

—QRUU UTBJGQ

**75**   WGULMWX KWTV I QGCKTMIW'V
QIJKKJ EIVUKJ ULIW JKXHAIJ VKF
IWT PKMWX MW AGYK.

—OIUUGW GVZIAU

**76**   C MSQILVC GQTCX GCU
IZBZXESW CIIZUEZV MQI
VILPLXN CIQKXV C UEQIZ
YCIDLXN SQE GLEA AZI EAIZZ-
WZCI-QSV NICXVVCKNAEZI
ULEELXN QX EAZ IQQM QM EAZ
CKEQTQFLSZ.

**77** UA U OCWZ'V OCIJCUB TI XCKJI

QPUJBPHHB WVCKBHS, U OHDJB

PCEX TXQHSX CZ XZLUZXXK HK C

WQUXZVUWV.

— QPKUWVHRPXK MZULPV,

CJUCW VE'W RXVXK TKCBI

**78** WUL DNHYGTDRM EDBH ULR WEH

RLSHI AYGOH GR HTLRLNGTM.

WEHC'YH WEH JGYMW WL

JGQPYH LPW DII LJ WEH IGWWIH

TEDYQHM LR WEHGY AELRH

SGII.

— XDC IHRL

**79** SDI PLPIFS W VDXGH TIJXFU

EIUIFSXFJ DXU CWEIFSU

VLXFVXHIU OXSD SDI PLPIFS

SDI CWEIFSU HISIEPXFI SDI

VDXGH XU FLO SLL DIWYK SL

VWEEK WFKPLEI.

**80** MBG CWHN XBH UFD YWDSH
OHHC HKQHONFRH OHM
AWJAHDN? BURH XBH QHWQEH
MH'RH AHHO AWJAFOL
WRHD XBH GHUDN AHHO
SWJQEUFOFOL?

—LHWDLH MUEEUSH

**81** H NMHSJ C YXXU RXM EX XSZJM
MJCPXE SZCE SX CWW SZMJJ XM
RXDM ZDEWMJW CLMJP SX VO
VCBEHRHLJES JPSCSJ.

—FCLU QXEWXE

**82** X'B AXOC TR NHSHOTXC....
X TRVQO VJXOA VJQ PHS XO
RSTOV TR BQ XG RTIITEXOL BQ
VJQ ITOL EHM HSTFOC.

—CQOOXG BXIIQS

**83** AFT BD BR RFCR, KLNH LSRHZ
RFCZ ZLR, RFH MHNDLZ AFL
HQIOHNCZRPT THPPD "RFCR'D
AFCR B'K RCPWBZ' COLIR!"
FCEZ'R DCBE CZTRFBZU RL RFCR
MLBZR?

**84** W'P IWCQ UH AYEQ CWPX.
W KQU UAHXQ LYUQVBYI
MQQIWBKX. IWCQ GAQB W'L
INWBK HB UAQ ZHDZA YBP W
ZYB'U VQYZA UAQ VQLHUQ
ZHBUVHI.

—CYUAIQQB LYPWKYB

**85** RYMDJD ECLOYLD NUHY XYYM
UAAUROYV XZ BYCBPY ANYZ'LY
ALZQMT AC QMAYLHQYE. MC
CMY OMCED NCE FUMZ.

—ICM DAYEULA

**86**   A OWEAB AB; A'E O
PRVUIPUSWYAOI. NCB A
EOSOZF BU IUSBYUJ AB LABP O
VJOIFNU.

—WFSSAD EAJJFY

**87**   LQYJ SX FWIF "FST XD XLYMHY
GDZJCF" DJ XQY FSCY DU XQY
GWRGYBF PDT, XQYI'BY JDX
MISJN. XQWX SF WMM XQDFY
XQSJNF LSMM QDMC.

—VYUU UDTLDBXQI

**88**   BWA OWQVZUAT OVTRATH IMO
M OVSSAOO. BWA ZQKQBQCH
PMFZAU.

—SQMSW CFGA UFBGM,
QD NVMTBATKMSG LFC
CSCMWQD'O QEATMBFQD

**89** ZDYWS A KWR W QGY-WMY-
SGJJDR KEMKGZ WMY ZNDETNZ
NDR AMKATMABAVWMZ A WU.
DB VDEQKG, A ZNDETNZ ZNWZ
SGKZGQYWS ZDD, WMY AZ
QWAMGY.

—RDDYS WJJGM

**90** RYDV U JP ZQNOD BYXR
UHPDQJNBDB RNJY JYD
FYQUBD "QNFFDH AQXO JYD
YDUHENVDB," HXDBV'J JYUJ
MGBJ ODUV JYD RQNJDQB
ZXGEHV'J ZXOD GF RNJY
UVLJYNVT XQNTNVUE?

**91** HOCT OGWJCN ICJJCF GN
KLOCJVG NK "SCN NOCC NK G
TDTTCUI!" OC WGI OGBC XCCT
DAVTS GT CJVMGXCNOGT AJGTS
HKUF EKU "XUKNOCJ."

**92** ONEESJKXX SX ONISJV N TNMVK,
TFISJV, QNMSJV, QTFXK-YJSC
BNUSTZ SJ NJFCOKM QSCZ.

—VKFMVK RHMJX

**93** NMDS XVDS KZZQ DLGZ PMF
UMXXZH V QCWOZ LC GZ. W
ELMXH DZZ WS KVDC'S V JZVX
UJLOZDDWLCVX NLA. SIZJZ KVD
AMSSZJ LC WS.

—JLHCZF HVCPZJOWZXH

**94** C'IH BMY CE QW DZEU HECFDZQ
ZEJ BMVVNHQ YLZY CY OCNN
PHHB YLH BKWTHQQWKQ AMQU
TWK XHEYMKCHQ ZKFMCEF WIHK
OLZY C DHZEY.

—RZDHQ RWUXH

**95**  DCOSZJ KFFZ MFRV-FYIRHEFA
VHB QFRR HOFB NQFZNE EFCBM
ZHQ, S DHRA NDF BFTHBA VHB
THZMFTPNSOF "FYIRHEFF HV
NDF YHZND" CQCBAM.

**96**  U BVP NRVCPO XL VEVJAUFV
AMJJOUCB PQV AXLLUCF XL WO
LJUVCZF SQX VEVJAUFV.

—JVZ FGVRPXC

**97**  GY UEQ QGQA'W NRAW IO WE
PRW VPRW, SP NEIHQ SRDP
VRQP LENO ZIA YROWPZ.

—RGOSR WXHPZ

**98**  KT DGFXMU BLP L PXCXGX WLPX
JD BTOJWBJMUGFL. BX VBFMEP
BX'P UXLU.

—WGLFI PBLGD

**99** NB OHBBC WM OBCVAVGB
ASSXO, NB TVYB UWMMBA
VCVAG, NB GVZB OBCVAVGB
YVJVGWSMO. NB'AB USWMF
BYBAIGTWMF NB JVM GS ZBBC
SEA XVAAWVFB GSFBGTBA.

        —ASUMBI UVMFBAQWBHU

**100** ESPQXGOSDU VDWRN
ESYDXYB AGS GZY QNSQGJY:
YUQXP JQDEY XG AWHH.

**101** GC LND JOOF BK TJDOYWNCGTF
CLNC GQ KTE CNXO N
UNYJEYOCTY NHNYC NFS HEC
GC CTMOCLOY NMNGF OFTEML
CGBOD, KTE IGZZ OWOFCENZZK
LNWO CIT TQ CLOB.

        —QYTB N ZOCCOY DOFC CT
          CLO "UNY CNZX" MEKD

**102** ZX YWX YUU ABWI KOYWCGIE,
MWXQO, YIJ QNBIVYIXBTQ, YIJ
CTQV AX KGLGUGSXJ AXMBWX ZX
YWX MGV VB NYWVGKGNYVX GI
QBKGXVF.

—RTJGVO "CGQQ
CYIIXWQ" CYWVGI

**103** Z XHNJ SOHN L GPYZXLU
LNJOZXLE SLNZUP. NJ, NP
NHGVJO, VJO GVZOC VBIQLEC,
VZI CLBWVGJO SOHN L IJXHEC
NLOOZLWJ, NP IGJYIZIGJO, VJO
ZUUJWZGZNLGJ IHE.

—XLOHU VJEOP

**104** WGEP ZYB LSU EB APKXPQ, CKX
S UGFX LSE, "OP AQYSUAYF CKX
EYFUSHFB." OYU KGU SK ULGWP
IGQXW.

—IGGXB CFFPK

**105** H YOGN NQ NPO NPHTNHONP
TORGHQG QZ DC ATOUSPQQI. H
WHWG'N YEGN NQ JQ LOSERUO
H'KO ARN QG, IHMO, QGO
PRGWTOW AQRGWU.

—YOGWC IHOLDEG

**106** HYPO NSI XVP XMSIJ JYCVJN-
ZCDP NPXVQ SEU, QSWPJYCOK
JPVVCMEP XEHXNQ YXFFPOQ JS
WIQCB.

—QJPDP VXBP

**107** QGFQND CJP AZC JQOC RU NRIH
EZMGP FMAZ Q BRFCG, DR AZQA
FZCJ NRI NCGG AZC JQOC FMGG
EQHHN.

—SMGG ERDSN

**108** XGT BW-DZKKZBO
RWUUEBMUTBX REUT ECXTJ EHTK
IEY YKEZB. IEY REZB SABZYGTM
CWJ RWUUZXXZBO EB ERX XGEX
IEYB'X PTX ZKKTOEK?

**109** NMPMDQZ FGQ YIZD BTAQ CP
GQBFDTOQZ. DJQP WM MID
TS VFTGZ, DJQP XJTSQ FD
STWJD, FSH DJQP WM FSPXJQGQ
DJQGQ'Z UMMH.

—ETBBP NGPZDFB

**110** ARC XS LE ARC TXTCF BXLS
"DLI BXMC! MXBA PCCV!" PRG
XSQCFALBC? L XMFCXSG ULBBCS
LA. ARCG'FC OJBA FJDDLEI LA
LE.

—GXVHQ BULFEHNN

**111** XAKQPRLWK RJZR QWJQ BK
BAOO OADK QWK RJSK OAHK,
FDKM JXG FDKM JCJAX. CFG,
A'OO WJDK QF RAQ QWMFYCW
QWK ALK LJNJGKR JCJAX.

—BFFGZ JOOKX

**112** KAO HCSCQOLO ACBO
XOBOFMSOX CQ CPKMICKOX
XMY-RCLAVQY ICDAVQO. VK'L
TCX RAOQ ZMP PQFMCX VK
CQX GVQX CQ OJKNC SCR KACK
XMOLQ'K ICKDA.

—DNCVY EVFTMNQ

**113** BO SNK ERNQ HZT IPTAIJT
FTAMNR BM MHKFBY, HZTR
ATIDBVT HZIH ZIDO IAT
MHKFBYTA HZIR HZIH.

—JTNAJT LIADBR

**114** D PDTQ DA ZCARGZ GCFI AK
WKZAZCI C SXFDTGFFBCT.
SGDTU SVCTQ, ZCARGZ EZXGV,
CTQ DTEKBWGAGTA EKBGF
TCAXZCVVI AK BG.

—HKRT EVGGFG

**115** AQFY E BCTWG TR GFTGPF BT
JYMT E CFOMEWCEYM EYX MQF
ZEJMCF X' EONO "QTA ZEYK ECF
KTW?" J ATYXFC JR ZWPMJGPF
GFCOTYEPJMJFO RJBWCF JYMT
MQF FHWEMJTY.

**116** HY KQ OGRCNNYCI ZGXCIAUQ KQ
DUXNYCO CXGNA CH OBXDXGON
KN TGCI U JUX, ZBC CINQ
KGOONA.

—CHK JHCCNX

**117** VOY CYGVPNV VBXC TY P FWPGC
TA VYYVO RV GPFOV, NB GBJ
EYSBWY P FB VB NXYYK P SPXX
TA TBIVO JPVO OBV JRVYW RGC
UBSSYY EYRGN.

— HYSS TRWCYW

**118** H LFZJ'M F WXBI DYYT
FSSYPJMFJM. H FULFIZ RXUM
MVFM HR IYP DYM LHMVHJ MLY
YB MVBXX QPSGZ YR HM, MVFM
LFZ SUYZX XJYPDV.

— QYQ JXLVFBM

**119** TVK SNUOABAUSUOL YE SNU
HYESUOSYAU. SNUK'OU AVZN
QBHUO SNUE.

— LBVXK LDQUL

**120** V JPWF SJF DNIU NT PR
FVMJSFFR-UFPA-NYI. V LFFX VS
VR SJF TAVIMF.

—OXVLF GVYYVMPR


**121** NSHSW FWVYNFHSRJN HJW
CWJWFE ZRFYSYOYHQN TDRNW
AHJPWNS NWOJWS ZJRDYXYSN
SDWC GJRC JIQQYQV GRJ
DYVDWJ RGGYOW.

—AWQQYN CYFFWJ


**122** E HPDC SD T YEPC, OHSZP SKK
YZEDBEDA TDY RPTMQ PTCEDA,
TDY ED KSNZCPPD YTQO E VSOC
CHS HPPBO.

—GSP P. VPHEO

**123** HJRK Y HUF ZYIIZR VEV HEOZW
VULR GJEGEZUIR AMEFIYKC,
UKW FJR'W ZRI VR ZYGL IJR
SRUIRMF. UKW IJRK FJR'W IOMK
IJRV EAA.

—VUMIQ GEJRK

**124** EKX IYKR EKX'UQ AQHHBYA KMS
RLQY EKX NHKKW HK HBQ EKXU
NLKQMFOQN FYS RKYSQU RLFH
QMNQ EKX OKXMS SK RLBMQ
EKX'UQ SKRY HLQUQ.

—AQKUAQ DXUYN

**125** AUBR FE XPQ LNYSXQQE-
PYEMSQMZ, CQNCJQ YZQM XN
KUJR USNYEM HNFEH, "XPFZ FZ
U JNEH XFIQ UHN."

—HFJAQSX HNXXLSFQM

**126** EDZA OBDOPB KDG'A SGDJ JXUA
AXBT'HB KDRGN. UGK U PDA DQ
AXBE UHB HBUPPT NDDK UA RA.

—NBDHNB LUHPRG

**127** VJI GXAUBIK MSVJ QTVF SF VJTV
VJIC RIV VJI FTKI INTQV BAAE
MJIVJIX VJIC FII T KAVJ AX TY TN
KDXLIXIX.

—GTDBT GADYLFVAYI

**128** UDEJXY DRDHC GZJKMHD JB
ZX FWWFHSMXJSC BFLDUFYC
OJBEDB SEDC EZY LJBBDY.

—KJKC SFLKJX

**129** ME FCYYOJ QEA FZHQ YQO NEXX
ULBOX IEZ, LT IEZ AEJB LM C
NCMB IEZ HCM'Y YCBO QEFO
XCFVUOX.

—OPPLO HCMYEJ

**130** 'UEL HDU IHDMTO UD OIAB UOI

KIIGAI MB, GMU UD LMBBDWU

OEY ZKUIW.

—LOZPILBIZWI, "UEYDH

DK ZUOIHL"


**131** AXMOGH VRF OGVFMQOFE

CTMVOTG TD BG FCOUTAF TD

B CTCXYBM VQ HBJF URTE,

B PTGVFUVBGV AFUPMOIFA

RFMUFYD BU B "UVBZ-BV-RTJF

JTJ." PYFBMYZ, URF EBU YZOGH.


**132** GQOVC VCFVC TV JGC JGTFB S

GQOVC GSV NGTWG ACCHV TJ

YOQL ZCJJTFB QF HCQHXC.

—N.W. YTCXUV

**133** O'H GFS NOMA YV PCK UFY
UOWW FJTS MYGFOMP JWW HK
WOVS, JMA GFSM GFSK'WW
AORBYTSL YOW UFOWS GFSK'LS
AOPPOMP HK PLJTS.

—PSYLPS PYQSW

**134** SZHL'R PXCHL HWETL HRVKXKQ
KR LZHL QE AHLLCX ZES FEQP
MET RTGB EQ KL, KL QCUCX
FERCR KLR DFHUEX.

—PXCPP XEPCFF

**135** O ZAUQXW VZ CUXQ IOYQ
CQ O LDUMUL IMORR KW. U
MURPQXQW PV UP ZVA ZUYQ
DVNAR SQZVAQ U AQOMUJQW UP
DOW O RKAOPKD VX UP.

—QCV LDUMULR

**136** A CGO'B FZVO BG XPGT GZC
XPVRJEQZZI. A FZVO BG KVSJ
EVRJZAEBM QOBAZ DI JVPM
DJJB.

— PABV PQCOJP

**137** NQVTV'I BROBDI PMV NVBWQVT
DPZ QBU B WTZIQ PM. YPT
HV LN'I HD OLYV'I BVTPXLWI
LMINTZWNPT.

— XTLBM GLRVD

**138** VQOFUV KBUH OMQ WNJKW
UN SQQF HUBXJG HNTQGOD,
FDJKW JK VNHXJUOFH GDJKW NS
KNUVJKW.

— MQGG SNYY

**139** P BZTM RHF H GMHOVPZM

HSBJY H ZMF SBBW SC H VBTHV

HJYGBX, IJXIBXYPZL YB SM

H RJXEPEHV LJPOM QBX YGM

MZO BQ YGM FBXVO. FGHY P'O

VPWM YB WZBF PR, PQ YGM

FBXVO MZOR, FGMXM FPVV YGM

RJXEPEBXR SM?

**140** DO TVA WEM PHQHQNHP GV

GEJH XDMJXV NDSVNE HRHPT

KET, TVA KVM'G MHHK DG.

　　　　　　　—HSSHM KHXHMHPHC

**141** G ISVA LO MSWIC QMGI KCCT.

G DSQ E HPCQQO DSSA HPGNC

USP GQ, YWQ GQ LEAC LO

VEJAVSPA LEA EI MCVV.

　　　　　　　—DEPPO IMEJAVGJD

**142** J ICYK YSL QM FASBHQWKGPA,
DAWUSURM EWA KGP RSYK
KJQP. YGP'Y BWK YJTN WA
SBMKGJBF, YGP ICYK UWAPY
KGP GPRR WCK WE QP.

—S. LGJKBPM UAWLB

**143** MUOMKY IX SGEX JQ KQCL
ERGUHLXS, IXEMCYX JRXK MLX
JRX QSXY ORQ OGUU ERQQYX
KQCL LXYJ RQDX.

—BRKUUGY HGUUXL

**144** JEVVJP MELG EZ H
GDSPAYHAMPV ODN WPAPHJ
VQP FHN YPZ ODN JEZXPAEP.
VQPN XPV GVDTT VQPN QHKP ZU
EZVPAPGV EZ RDGV VU XPV VQP
SAECP EZGELP.

—RPTT TUIFUAVQN

**145** INN BYCIOLYCX PLXO NCIYU
OM BMCJFXO. OGIO'X KGH
OGC TYMKU TCIY IUZ OGC
DFCNZ PMLXC BIU ... NFWC FU
GIYPMUH. MD BMLYXC OGCH
BIU'O PIOC, MY OGC PFBC
KMLNZ CJANMZC.

—TCOOH KGFOC

**146** UGC VLBBNJNQGWMC
UPFUGJQP WQJXGSMSTC NV
NGPNVWNGTLNVXUYMQ BZSH
HUTNJ.

—UZWXLZ J. JMUZAQ

**147** NF TXUFUPYMH YM NF TZETVH
LQU LYRR AFUL HUPUVVUL LQD
HQT HQYFJM QT EVTGYXHTG
DTMHTVGND GYGF'H QNEETF
HUGND.

—TONF TMNV

**148** UF UQU ... MJVRX UR JC XBO
BL CGR UQTLBLE JLN XJFX,
"CGR RJTYF KBTN SJCSGRX CGR
MQTU." BI B MJLC J MQTU,
... B'YY NTBLV J KQCCYR QI
CRPWBYJ.

—AJU XCQLR

**149** GYJUV UT Y OCJUEO VH
CBLCGLYUBOCBL ZIUXI DCGOULT
OUKKUVBT VH DCVDKC LV
KUTLCB LV LIC TYOC FVMC
YL LIC TYOC LUOC, YBJ SCL
GCOYUB KVBCTVOC.

—L.T. CKUVL

**150** SP RQU ZESWSPVA KZOSU, RQU
SPOSCSLAU KVP KYCR LU PVMUT
RZ CRVI YPCUUP ... LYR VC QU
EYPC RQEZYWQ RQU CPZF, QU
AUVOUC CQZUNESPRC.

**151** BDU RQZUTDBBD X DBZXIUC

R IMYTIM'N NZRXDUC HERNN

AXDCBA RDC, ZMU ARL ZMU

NYDEXHMZ MXZ XZ, X ABYEC'SU

NABTD XZ EBBWUC OYNZ EXWU R

HTXEEUC IMUUNU NRDCAXIM.

**152** NMXV HQQS LQIG VWIMPXSG

WAKW WAQG VAMRSN KSFKGV

XM FTWA GMR TP WAQ OKI, TP

OKVQ WAQ PQQN VAMRSN KITVQ

HMI WAQJ WM CKIZ LTMSQPWSG

KW PMWATPX ITXAW TP GMRI

QKI.

— NKLQ CKIIG

**153** IZUUPMI EQDDPZJ PL Q RBU

RPCZ IZUUPMI PMUB Q UGS BO

XBU HQUZD. QOUZD NBG IZU

GLZJ UB PU, PU QPM'U LB XBU.

— EPMMPZ KZQDR

**154** VKBP WK ZDTIWLZ JV QT NFVS

ZC SBZLTN QWCF BWDWCTJ

SZIEWKA, VXTISIWLTJ WCTDN,

ZKJ BVKA BWKTN ZKJ LZBB CFTD

LVKXTKWTKLT NCVITN.

— PZEVX NDWIKVUU


**155** ABMY BAD'P YSYGHPUBDW. PUY

NUFQY BA YDZFDWYGYZ, NUBQY

PUY FDP EJDPBDLYA PJ ZJ VLAP

RBDY.

— IBQQ SFLWUFD


**156** N UGGJ CX WIGGR. N CVOG

UH EHUGW VEHDY NY. N UGGJ

GNQSY SHDTW V JVX, VUJ VY

IGVWY YGU VY UNQSY.

— ENII SNFOW

**157** VNB AGX GRUGVZ FCTCXF NX
YPC GJCKQAGX TCNTRC YN
FN YPC KQHPY YPQXH—NXAC
YPCV'DC CMTRNKCF GRR YPC
NYPCK TNZZQIRQYQCZ.

—UQXZYNX APBKAPQRR

**158** T SE SB MKWBCKSCDU LTCV
BJPTDCG SB S ZGKJESRTSP TR S
ZDCKTMTDU MJKDBC.

—S. LVTCRDG AKJLR

**159** QT COXH OJ FW HFNKI JOUW;
O'Q F CFKHN JOUW. KDUHKIHN
CH QFZH QVP.

—NDPWHT PFWUHNXOHAP

**160** L'I ZXSLQF JYIYRLXH IXZP OV
L TXQ PYHU IG OVQ IXSY LZ ZV
ZPY ZPLJR FJXRY.

—OLQDXR

**161** I TLRLXY RHCLJ TVGGHNLN AHYQ

I WJHZVX KIX. RVYVJHZYZ IJL

IZPLN YV DL VX YQL GVVPVFY

OVJ ZHCYLLX QIJNLXLN

TJHRHXIGZ.

— JVXXHL TVJDLYY


**162** Y EHP'N NZYPC QO HPRNZYPL

VQFW ZQFFYAIW NZHP BZHFYPL

XZHN Y'V GQYPL HII GHR.

— FWPWW DWIIXWLWF,

FW NXYNNWF


**163** JDIFZ LZGG RA VNAE LDQRPK ET

GRAEZP ET TNC KCDPWHDCZPEA

FCZDELZ ELCTNKL ELZRC

PTAZA MLZP ELZI'CZ ZDERPK

ADPWMRXLZA.

— VRJ XDCCZI

**164** NIJVA NIUN CJPYO TWQA PL
AVVAFNWUY YWSADNB NJ TUWF
U YWNNYA NAZLJDUDB VUXANB
OAVADQA FAWNIAD.

—SAFMUZWF XDUFRYWF

**165** UDIA GMJ DFKI TIS GMJC
PMRG IXNWT F DMCXMAI WDFW
RCNYWT RMUA WDI DFHH NAWM
GMJC QDNHR'T CMMX FAR XFZIT
WDIX UFAW F RCNAZ MY UFWIC.

—LIYY YMSUMCWDG

**166** K PMUZ RSMVV UXFBR OZJMLRZ
XBJZ CXL'YZ RZZB UPZ JMBBXB
KB UPZ EMQG UPZQZ'R
BXUPKBH ZVRZ UX IX.

—VZBBC OQLJZ

**167** VUIKUWK CVBKA IK, "SZCM'V

PUFJ GAKC UX C DUUA MGIK?" G

VCGA, "VGL XUJMP-XGOK."

—AGTB TCOKMM


**168** XY YZMQYU-YZQDD WMODR, YZD

OCBHDRY WXMB RYQDDY MB YZD

EBMYDV RYXYDR MR MB MROXBV

FXQP, MVXZC.


**169** MBFBQ JBBU AU XNHY HYB

DZMBTBT. PQRV HYBO PZXM HZ

GZAQ EBFBE; NH'T LYBRUBQ.

—IABMHNM LQNTU


**170** GDTU JRXHZVDK CRFZUV

KZIT CKRQKC, QRJZS RUJ KF

RUUSBUETQC RJFZCT BC KDRK

GT GZHH HSCT RU DSBQ SP

CHTTN. Z JSU'K. Z HSCT RU

DSBQ SP JSZUV CKBPP.

**171** G'N YDEEGLY BDWV

QANKAWEHOZD TGES NV OAJV.

G'N UZDDIGLY AL H KXZZ-

ZDLYES NGWWAW.

—UHLJWH ODWLSHWJ

**172** BKDLCHDLB H YKJRLW YQLCQLW

CQL YKWPR HB VLHJU WMJ

VI BDOWC NLKNPL YQK

OWL NMCCHJU MB KJ KW VI

HDVLXHPLB YQK WLOPPI DLOJ

HC.

—DOWT CYOHJ

**173** L FBYRM DA DVT FLV XT HLWJBH

VDH HD MD FTSHLYV HBYVJU,

UWFB LU HDWFB L BDH UHDZT,

OWRR RLKOU DAA DA HLXRTU,

LVM CLQT KDKKG XTADST VDDV.

—IDLV SYZTSU

**174** PQM KMAP JUE PS TSAM JMBXQP

BA PS ITSAM ESLC VSLPQ,

ASVMPQBFX GMCE WBYYBILTP

YSC U HSTBPBIBUF.

— MW ZSIQ

**175** MYRNIB Y ZMNSC NU UXKQSO

VMQ HAUV WQYXVNDXS

NKKYVNAIYS YZV VMYV VLA

GQAGSQ NI SARQ ZYI ZAHHNV.

— WNSS ZAUWO

**176** XBBAJYHH DBKJOILF AML

ATB TBGFA XLYASGLF BX

YKLGODYI HOXL: WOBHLIDL YIE

DBKKOAALL KLLAOIQF.

— QLBGQL TOHH

**177** LPG AKCQDCVZ JU C XJYKEGM
LPCL PCF DGGE LJJ QGOO
SOCEEGA HF LPCL HL AJGF
EJL OGCWG GEJYRP KJJN UJK
CAWGELYKG.

— CEAKG RHAG

**178** SC TEOFXUZ JFOF NXUFRRNKFXU,
FXRNKLUFXFQ TFGTRF. ULFC
EWWFTUFQ SF VGO JLEU N JEZ: E
TBXNZLSFXU VOGS KGQ.

— QEPNQ ZUFNXYFOK

**179** IGFQ DEQFDEIFDOBVK YEHU
FCB MWBIDQB SHSBEF FCBDW
HUEBWQ UDVV GUGYBE, GEL
FCBE FCBK UGYB FCBS FBE
SDEJFBQ QHHEBW.

— ADS LGODQ

**180** YK S RBXXD GSW'O KSUU
SRUXXD, MBSO NFXR YO
GFAWO? SWN BFM GSW KYRB
RUXXD RF DXSGXKAUUV MYOB
SUU OBFRX NXSN JFQROXCR
SCFAWN?

**181** PSS EQX DIIY HG HUDQOPDVI
PDY VQDBHYIDVI, PDY FAID
GXVVIGG HG PGGXOIY.

— NPOT FKPHD

**182** T DCTOU TW ZKU NMCWTWI
ZMCW HUZXUUW ZKU LUOTCU
ZM TNSCMJU ZKU XMCAL DWL D
LUOTCU ZM UWFME ZKU XMCAL.
ZKTO NDRUO TZ KDCL ZM SADW
ZKU LDE.

— U.H. XKTZU

**183** G NRBL OT MUPO OT QB U
DTNPOZI-MBROBZP RGPHBZ,
QNO G OTTC U OBRO UPL G JUL
OTT WNDJ RBXY-BROBBW.

—QZBOO QNOXBZ

**184** XCJPJ WNKJB T XZKJ ECJG DNF
BCNFIH BXNU JQUJWXZGL NXCJP
UJNUIJ XN KTRJ T YZL HJTI
TYNFX DNFP YZPXCHTD. XCTX
XZKJ ZB TLJ JIJSJG.

—HTSJ YTPPD

**185** CNS KOP ZIUU DZ'F ZGI
KGJDFZTOF FIOFNP. FZNJIF OJI
FIUUDPE NXX ZGIDJ IVMDJIH
TDUL OF IEEPNE.

—HORDH UIZZIJTOP

**186** URT DPHJQTX SAUR OABUAHK AI

URGU AU XZIU ITTX BPTCAJQT,

SRAQT PTGQAUN ITQCHX AI.

—AIGJTQ GQQTKCT

**187** XGPPGNA LSYYJV (NFHSV

XLS YPNZJT YJVVZ ANRSO'R

Y.G. NGTJ SO HB) GR NO

NONWVNA SM YLGPGY ANVPSXJ

(MGFHGSONP RPJCHL GO

VNZASOT FLNOTPJV'R OSBJPR).

**188** ACVMNEO KVMC MZE PWNBZRC V

OCERGCKVE. TCGNCUNEO FQVR

QC ACVM KVMC QNK KVM.

—OCZAOC TCAEVAM XQVF

**189** PXOU RA NPU LMQGU FPUKU,

FPUH VXS PQBU NX DX NPUKU,

NPUV PQBU NX NQTU VXS RH.

—KXZUKN CKXAN

**190** OSTQ Y UTT B IAI RBNNKYQV

STN KAPQV RSYZG YQ AQT

AJ LSAUT OTBNBEZT "EBEK

SBNQTUUTU" Y LSYQC,

"OBUQ'L QYQT IAQLSU TQAPVS

BZNTBGK?"

**191** EPS TXL TL JQOTETVU EPS

VXJ. T PJISV'E PJO EPTL NQGP

EXAQMZS BTGRTVU LTOSL LTVGS

EPS TXJV-TXJF YJX.

— MTZZ NJPSX

**192** XCRPR MNZCX XM VR GH DGG

PRSNWPRTRHX XCGX JPIWHZ

VGVWRU CGOR XM ZM WHXM XCR

MORPCRGQ JMTYGPXRHX.

— VMVVI UKGIXMH

**193** KYDX FRX CL XNB MRKVY LCFY,

CK YDOZF XNB QDORI, KN LROO

RFODDZ. MYCVY DIZORCEF MYX

C ROMRXF ANPD NLL MYDE C'H

FENQTDOCEJ.

—DOODE ADJDEDQDF

**194** WFT'X ZF XF V EYSFFA PMDTCFT.

XSMPM'AA RM V AFX FQ FAW

OMFOAM XSMPM YAVCNCTZ XF

RM GFDP YAVEENVXME.

—XFN WPMMEMT

**195** Q VMB VYYZC YI CMQWQTG

UJ VYYZCJYFGC. BYM WUI'J

NGJ JSGH UJ JSG EQVFUFB,

VGWUMCG RGYREG TYI'J FGJMFI

JSGH.

—ZGOQI IGUEYI

**196** XZHA UHPBHI MQKBHIKKIK DZJI

VPUKIT, MQS SDI BHSICHIS

KSBPP UYYICK ZMQHTZHS

UWSBUHK SU TBKVCBXBHZSBHL

KDUWWICK, ZK PUHL ZK EDZS

SDIA EZHS BK WUCH.

—JZHVI TILIHICIK


**197** H KZR BJOOHYB P-RUZY ZYE OFJ

FSCJ RFSUUHYB YJOKSWG SY OFJ

RZCJ ROZOHSY. H ZPOIZMMN

LSIBFO Z PSYBWJRRCZY.

—LWIPJ LZIC


**198** HN DKY WOWI QJGL LK LKILYIW

FD CJC, LHW PHF YX JGC IHZPL

HG NIKGL KN PHF, IWNKRC J

IKJC FJX HGTKIIWTLRD.

—TJLPD RJCFJG

**199** BEKL JZ RWRVXLEJMA JQ KM

JDDTQJPM KMN MPLEJMA

RYJQLQ? JM LEKL GKQR, J

NRZJMJLRDX PWRVCKJN ZPV UX

GKVCRL.

— BPPNX KDDRM

**200** K WMB'H QUU HSU TMKBH ML

HUQHKBE VMQGUHKVQ MB

IPCCKHQ, CUVPYQU HSUX'IU

POIUPWX VYHU.

— IKVS SPOO

**201** ZQ ZG ODEDA'G QME

DIDXGEZXZGN OD'J UII KD

OUGXTZAW GDIDFZRZMA KN

XUAJIDIZWTG.

— WDMEWD WMKDI

**202** Y ZGU'B KTKU VNEUGAFKZLK
KVCBW ZVR. Y IYUZ YB
KJNKKZYULFR SYULGYPBYN VUZ
DXYBK XUIVYC BG BWK GBWKC
MFVUKBP.

**203** H'K EIAYDZ. HY C LCBIHYS OAHB
H XPPD XHDR C LCWBXRBB JRCW
UHBI C WALLRW LCYG CWPAYG
HB.

—GWRU ECWRZ

**204** O KNC'A JIROITI QNW Y EIBNCK
ASYA FIOZSAROQAOCZ OE Y
EXNWA. ASIH XOBV LX Y SIYTH
ASOCZ YCK XLA OA KNFC YZYOC.
AN GI, ASYA'E OCKIBOEONC.

—XYLRY XNLCKEANCI

**205** AO GL-JXDFRDXGSV ...

DGAXSVGV AG UR CPG YZPXSL

HGBKWYG YPG QKY MGDO

AOYCGDXUWY KSV GCGDSKF KSV

YUFXV, KSV PGD SUYG QKY YPUC

URR HO RDGSBP YUFVXGDY.

—GAU ZPXFXZY


**206** NW ROCGGUO VDB ECHOW'G

ECS OWDBKE ZDPPOO BWGNU

VDB ZCW GEJOCS C ROANWK

QCZENWO AENUO NG'R

JBWWNWK.

—MOPP IOXDR


**207** R XAZP QC HC ERAJRVH XVQRW

CVZ PNB RQ AQFXYM GZ: BCX

YNV DXB ERAJ. TJNQ QJZ JZWW

NG R PCRVH RV N DCNQ NQ

ECXF-QJRFQB RV QJZ GCFVRVH?

—MZVVB FCHZFACV

**208** Y BNH N BYSQ YQ N MRHRAIF
BULIR HYQXLH, "RNIB ZYRIPRX
HOYAR FLT HNYU." UOR
NAURIQNUYDR BUNSSRIB UOR
YCNSYQNUYLQ.

—RCYAF ARDYQR

**209** HMLK YML OVPLAKULKY BLYB
FN X NAVOAXU QLBZOKLQ YV
DALXYL YMVFBXKQB VG IVCB,
ZY KLPLA ZKPVEPLB BRZEEB Z
MXPL. HMLAL'B YML GLQLAXE
DVFKDZE GVA CXQ IVRL
HAZYZKO?

**210** TDFTUD VDDT QDUURCW AM
"QYDID RM CF R RC 'QDXZ.'"
LAQ GFA SXC MCXT QYD QFT
TRDSD FJJ QYD Q XCO ZXVD FCD.

**211** U NZCEHJ NQL NZSHC

NHXJ HFHCUCW WZNCK PZ

CUWQPMOTIK. NQL EZC'P PQHL

NHXJ CUWQPWZNCK?

—WHZJWH MXJOUC


**212** WX DJT UIY I ZFHHD IHY

OUGFV WO JXX OUF FRZWGF

MOIOF LTWKYWHB IHY WO UWO

MJRFLJYD WH OUF UFIY, WO

VJTKY QWKK UWR. OIKQ ILJTO

BFOOWHB DJTG RJHFD'M VJGOU.

—UFDVJJY LIHQM


**213** B SID'X ARGP RDKXABDO

RORBDWX LRVPNBLXW, UMX

B XABDY BX'W XBFP XI WXIQ

ZAPD KIM NIIY QPTFRDPDXNK

LTBOAXPDPS.

—WMWRD DITLNPPX

**214** YH IUWAUK ... KQL KUQBRIN

Q AUXYUG, LAMJXPUB WQPL,

EIUUWQPL, NXMFUL, QIP

LQHRIN, "R'Y NMIIQ BRPU YH

OREU." KAUBU? GABMJNA Q

YRIUVRUXP?

—KQIPQ LHEUL

**215** R YPZ D BON OBFRBO RB KM

LDW JPZ HRHB'Z ZDIO ZCO GSH

GBO GPZ. BGN KM LDW FGOQ

ARTO CPBHWOH KRSOQ DB

CGPW.

—QZOTOB NWRFCZ

**216** CA C QXY MGAJBOMJT, AJDD

AUJS PXH'BJ TMDDMGF AX

FMOJ C UHGLBJL CGL AJG

KJBZJGA. HGDJEE AUJ QXY ME

EACAMEAMZMCG.

—CLCS FBXKSCG

**217** KY KO YGIUM L OTLAX JTXC

MPIG OXWXC-MXLG-PUN OPC

OLMO, "NLNNM, JKUU MPI

STXSD AM ALYT?" LCN MPI TLWX

YP UKX LCN OLM, "K YGIOY MPI,

OPC."

—OKCVLN


**218** LUU QXV LOG UIKB CGUCKG HOU

AIUH OUH LU WZI LOG MUZILWB

XWG QZDB VWRSRIY MXQD XIV

MZLLRIY OXRW.

—YGUWYG QZWID


**219** CNJ EY LNA WZGZLMQJ EF Z

KHXWEV XHEWREFB VZWWAR LNA

"QAYLQMMI"? RMAY ZFJXMRJ

BM EF LNAQA UHYL LM LZOA Z

QAYL?

**220** I XBC IYB GAPFB HX JL
XBHYREPFRPPN RIN I NHGTQIL
HX ARB CHXNPC, QIEBQBN
"BGGBXAHIQ PHQG." H QPPVBN
ARBJ PKBF IXN NBUHNBN,
"XP, ARBL'FB XPA—H UIX NP
CHARPSA ARBJ."

**221** LCD OGPL ROHGILKSL LCRSB R
ZDKISDM YIGO XKLTCRSB [LCD
LN PCGX "TGHP"] RP, LCD GSD
XKU LG KNGRM FDRSB KIIDPLDM
RP LG XDKI K PCRIL.

       —MDSSRP IDBKS

**222** VSZTZ'R XJ RWMS VSFXP OR LWX
LJT VSZ USJQZ LOCFQD. VSZTZ
OTZ XJ CORROPZ EOTQJTR UFVS
FMZ MTZOC OXG LTZZ IZUZQTD.

       —IZTTD RZFXLZQG

**223** WSB MTOZDOB EPLZUX SU DEO
XANDE BZJ ZUB TOXDOB SU DEO
XOROUDE. DEAX ONYGZAUX Z
GSD. ESH WSSB AX JSPT SPDYPD
ZD DEO OUB SQ DEO HSTFHOOF?

**224** XGW FXG VOA RXG UYPJQ
EXNQTW VOPTQ CPEEPGM
X IYQSSW MPYT PE EPFITW
GAS MPJPGM SOQ CPEE SOQ
XSSQGSPAG PS UQEQYJQE.

—XTDQYS QPGESQPG

**225** AZSJ KU KJ ASG TSJG AZH
KLNVLJVB JVTZLHXHFD? AHRXB
JZVD ZSNV JN GZHAG GJSCCKLF
CRIIVC GPRVSW JHDG?

—BHRFXSG THREXSLB

**226** X'S EXIIXGN ZB MJJ WVPQJV

XG BKV MYFBBIM, XR QBK'VJ

EXIIXGN ZB RXGA P WIPYJ RBV

PINJHVP XG BKV YFKVYFJM.

—AQIPG HVBAQ


**227** QK HKTKB ZXWYKV, AN LXAFWN.

QK ISAACHFIXZKV UN RCZZFHE

XHH WXHVKBO XBZFIWKO SH

ZMK BKLBFEKBXZSB.

—DCVN ESWV


**228** G SAQW WV UIRN XVIJ RQF

WZGAF WV CLVVW ON RXA, KYW

G CLVW ON SAGXLW GQCWARF.

—KVK LVUA


**229** JX OZENFLNDWOVPX ANUBLBEB

NR RLKT PZUQWTQ FYOUI

VODTB. LE'B AOYYTQ "JT: EPT

ZUENYQ BENWX."

**230** ... T ZWF WFGOM HX AOMX
ED WBHXYTXLAWJKD WF W
YAXWMZWD EBFTRWP. T LXH FX
OCRTHOM T RXBPMV'H RXEJXFO
EDFOPU.

**231** QZ FWYLOQHVQPOP LVB
YJHDGOQHVQPOP RHOM OHHX
L KHHB MLWB DHHX LO L
SDLOUSGP, OMYU'B LKWYY
OMYWY CGPO RY L OMQWB
YTSDLVLOQHV.

**232** LNUP AX PNK BARRKJKHMK
YKPLKKH U PUZABKJIAXP
UHB U PUZ MESSKMPEJ? PNK
PUZABKJIAXP PUGKX EHSC CEOJ
XGAH.

                              —IUJG PLUAH

**233** ZXTLAVAIZXT XZMDLNA
CLYCPXV, TLRIDPNCPIX IR CQL
ANPX RIALYCY, CIUPM SNYCL
... PR CQL SIADT SLAL N EPV
NWNACKLXC, SL SIZDTX'C VLC
IZA TLWIYPC ENMB.

—HIQX AIYY

**234** O KFBBGY WTG MCJKTOK
HLOGIYC TDWBOIG. QG CMDEG
HDL COA TDXLC, FIY CTG YOYI'W
LGFBOPG WTFW O QFCI'W UDOIU
WD MFJ SJ NOBB.

—SOKTFGB FLDIOI

**235** V FOAXPZVL JOOJ LEO HMVJJ
XN RVLOZ VJ EVMN-NBMM; V
ZOGBKMSPVT ... RXTFOZJ REX
LEO EOMM FZVTQ EVMN ESJ
HMVJJ XN RVLOZ.

—WONN POJVZSX

**236** GI HSWFZPRV R-XCPZR XJFKSO:

"MCI XCFLJU P XSI VEALXV

GV MCVO IFL MVZV RCV FOV

DJFATPOK RCV MSI?" PR'X

YZPORVU FO RCV DSAT XF

YVFYJV ASO ZVSU PR SHRVZ P

XCFWV RCVG SXPUV.

**237** YNVFTJQWP RWQ ULERHULO NTW

SINAQ PNYUQJD. U KTPJ PRS R

JRJJNN FRWANW RHEQWJUPULO

JIRJ UJ IRP PFQAA-YIQYX.

—KRD AQLN

**238** ADUASD ZED UL "IJNMVJS

KJMGDG," ASMVJS. ZU NFDO

JSHJOG HUVR EI NJIZDC?

JVD NFDO EIZEXEZMJSSO

EIGMLLEKEDIN NU RESS?

**239** ZN ITXH LRTCVA T'Z LQQ CQAN.
OL MHOAL LROL'A IROL ARH
VHHEA ISTLTCU TC RHS WTOSN.

—WSOVH AOLRHS

**240** IUL OCKN D HF AKIN PKWCPH
DZCRH D VPQGQADE DH EDPXK
DEIDLN OKNVPQZK IUDH
IQHAKNNKN NDI UQG IKDPQAX?
Q ZKH UK'N UDO WEKAHL CY
HQGK HC VUDAXK ZL HUKA.

**241** HP XUM VUQ'Z RIEHICI
ZKTZ TBIGHJT HA TQZH-
HQZIEEIJZMTE, ZKIQ NKX HA HZ
ZKTZ UQ "DHEEHDTQ'A HAETQV"
ZKI JKTGTJZIG NKU KTV ZKI
NUGAZ RHEEHQD NTA ZKI
OGUPIAAUG?

—RHEE BTKIG

**242** NKR BMZSHRI ALNK
OVRIBHZTIRVN LX NKPN NKR
ILVONR TZO APWR OB LV NKR
IZMVLVU, TZO'MR ZV NKR GZS.

—XHPBBT AKLNR

**243** R TXHJVKV UVKCROURJC HJ BM
JVHLXDZUXZZI XRI RJ HCVB ZJ
CXVHU KSVTHRPK BVJO TRPPVI
"FVLVCRUHRJ TXHTAVJ." XZG
IZVK CXRC GZUA, VNRTCPM?

**244** A USY'Q NAGF PSVYQZM
LVJAP, RVQ A USY'Q LFOY QS
UFYAEZOQF QCSJF KCS US. OYU
XSZ QCF DFSDNF KCS NAGF
PSVYQZM LVJAP, UFYAEZOQF
LFOYJ "DVQ USKY."

—RSR YFKCOZQ

**245** OTLVTO, XFWWKXT CKF JTOT LD
HVHKI. LDV XFWWKXT CKF JTOT
L STSETO KZ MKDNOTXX. EFI H
OTWTLI SCXTUZ.

— SLOY IJLHD


**246** J SKH PKJHFT UA YQHR OA OXO.
OA NKRIFP TJFT SIFD J SKH
FJLIR AFKPH XBT. KR BFKHR,
RIKR'H SIKR IF RXBT QH JD RIF
BFRRFP.

— TPFS VKPFA


**247** NCP YXBD WC LDIDIODL CED
WYSEJ XOCPW WYD HSMM CG
WYD FDCFMD: SW HXUE'W WYXW
MCEJ XJC WYXW HD HDLD UHDFW
XHXN ON WYD IXKXLDEX.

— QCE UWDHXLW

**248** I MWLBPO HB I BANNWBB HZ FW

TWEB AM HO EFW KPLOHOT IOQ

TWEB EP VWQ IE OHTFE IOQ HO

VWEDWWO QPWB DFIE FW DIOEB

EP QP.

—VPV QGUIO


**249** MGW RSUM OKXMXLM WIXRBKW

SQ ZNEWKMT MS XLCRXKU CU

MGW NSMCUUWNCW. CM'U FEUM

X NWXKKT RSNOCP QWNNCU

JGWWK QSN ZGCZVWLU.

—RCMZG GWPOWND


**250** BLFY BYY H THGZ JWLNT HET

WLLZ KLG XUY BCWAYG WCECEV.

PUYE XUYS TL, C GYFCET XUYF

XUHX BCWAYG XHGECBUYB.

**251** GJ ZLV VLYEU'O VYEOALF
ILBBFCLLV PLDBYWRAV, IY
LCYE ELVLN RUV ZLNLAARI RU
RHLBLZF.

—KRF BYUL

**252** D KIONP AE LBAWAUZBK
OKODXXP QLGLDXK ISDI ISL
VLKI IZUL IA VOP DWPISZWY ZK
XDKI PLDQ.

—UDQIP DXXLW

**253** FD IWCVMEZ ... YRLV RM W
CVERCVFVME JNFFBMRED, KTRJT
RZ GWZRJWYYD W FRMRFBF-
ZVJBCRED ICRZNM KRET W XNYU
JNBCZV.

—ONVY KWCZTWK

**254** Y XNZC MZBXLBJVWYZQ CBWJF.
XNGG, JDCRJGGF Y XNZC
DJVNNZYZQ BEE J UBRZCJYZ BZ J
QYJZC CBZQRN WNSVNMMBV.

— SJRG SVBANZIJ

**255** L CFFZ Y CIF-GPYA-FJN
HFBUWCPA LM CF OP APUYLAPN,
YMN CQP TWG JFFZPN YC BP YK
CQFWTQ QP IYK Y TWM NPYJPA
YMN L'N OAFWTQC QLB Y
BWKZPC.

— RFM KCPIYAC

**256** SW TIB MGZ XW IXFW ZG
JTIRJMW DGS GOL FJUWE VGOFQ
XW TGLW PLOEZLIZJMR IMQ
VGTHFWC, XOZ VGMRLWEE VIM.

— VOFFWM DJRDZGSWL

**257** O BX HNAXYBN HNJ

AJCAOBJAUHXA IX LUQZ HOLJI

UH QOBNH LZ QJOBNVXAI

HNOQD EJ NURJ U IHAXVJ TOBNH

OQ HNJ DOHPNJQ.

—LUK UTJKUQFJA


**258** QRX HUJ NRZIJ BTHN, ZYTZVP

SHVOFJI SHTTJO GZLVOI, QRJV

FN'I NRJ HTGZVO DZXI NRHN

RHKJ GZLVOI FV NRJG?


**259** L WYEIJBVCYE VRI LYAIYVGJ

GS VRI KCQTLTIB NCB LYBTLJIE

NRIY RI BCN C OCY MCJJFLYQ

CY LYELQYCYV, CBVROCVLM TLQ

WYEIJ RLB CJO.

—CXSJIE RLVMRMGMP

**260** LON CMDCSEN SQ IGENIGHH
XE LS ELGFV XF SFN CHGAN
QSD ES HSFY LOGL CNSCHN
YNL ES ISDNV LONJ'HH CGJ LNF
VSHHGDE QSD G INND.

—ELNCONF ASHINDL

**261** VYJB LWINZHJ RWCGJG RBS
LYCBDG HIIX ZRS, LYJWJ CG
RHVRPG IBJ CBSCACSNRH VYI
UJWTJCAJG R GIHNLCIB RBS
CG VCHHCBD LI LRXJ TIEERBS.
AJWP IOLJB, LYRL CBSCACSNRH
CG TWRQP.

—SRAJ ZRWWP

**262** KSV BHD JK JVQQ BXVS DKL'GV
XHYFSI HS VHGJXOLHAV FP DKLG
CVQQ-K PJHSWP PJFQQ.

—PKLZD PHQVP

**263** LDCFC'A AE QRND SEIIRLPEU
PU LDC TPF UEM LDTL PW
PL MCFCU'L WEF ERF IRUZA,
LDCFC'B JC UE SITNC LE SRL PL
TII.

—FEJCFL EFJCU

**264** G ZNSM BGHMX MBQFGQUR
CZMU G IMWMGSM BP ONFZMI'R
XNP TGOFR. G'B TYNX BP
WZGYXIMU IMBMBVMI BM; G'B
XGRNLLQGUFMX FZNF FZMP
FZGUD G XIMRR YGDM FZNF.

—BGDM XJTNU

**265** OSVJ CNC UMWIJ OZNYV
"SVM, AZ. YIACNTZGJV AIJ,
KWIM I HNJF XNZ AV," UGU GY
NDDTZ YN SGA YSIY MNT DIJ'Y
IDYTIWWM KWIM I HNJF NJ I
YIACNTZGJV?

**266** IVB YSVZ GM'C MGPX MV NV VS

U QGXM ZFXS IVB'AX CMUSQGSN

SXRM MV IVBA LUA USQ NXM U

MGLYXM DVA QVBEHX-TUAYGSN.

—MVMGX DGXHQC

**267** GYWTW YMXW CWWK GALWD

IYWK A'L DGQFZ HK GYW

JTWWIMN MKP A GYAKZ GH

LNDWEJ, "AJ YMEJ GYW FAGN

PAWP TARYG KHI, A'P CW YHLW

METWMPN."

—VMQE TWADWT

**268** T LF XFN KPUTPHP TX WX

WGNPMUTGP, WUNYFDBY T

WO KMTXBTXB W EYWXBP FG

DXLPMQPWM.

—QFFLJ WUUPX

**269** L XWVO VXO RWILSC "WTEWIR
W DALUORZWLU, SOPOA W
DALUO." L TLHO VQ NJV LV LSVQ
NOARNOYVLPO DI VXLSHLSC
"WTEWIR W NWTTDOWAOA,
SOPOA W YQANRO."

—TWJAW HLCXVTLSCOA

**270** EDOZN, VIJ CHTHWH VIDV LDTJE
NSB ZSST EZHLLJM IDE NJV VS
CJ HWAJWVJO.

—JZHQDCJVI IBMZJN

**271** LC NWQFPY KHZPHQPO QFP
IAYSBWY WBWYL, RFKVF
AHNJYQAHWQPBC RWM MQJBPH
NYJL FKL.

—ZKVQJY IJYSP

**272** Z COIL TXORYL U JYZYOUYOU.

ZL'I LYF KXR WXA EUNS VFXVEF.

SXO KXD'L YUHF LX PUEQ ZL.

COIL YXEK ZL XOL LYF PZDKXP

UDK IGOFFNF.

—UDLYXDS JEUAQ

**273** EDYX EIM "FIT WE UDJ JOX

IUEFXT." AXKXUAE DU JOX

BRXEJWDU ... WV EDYXDUX

IEZE "FOIJ WE TIF EKXQQXA

GIHZFITAE?," VDT XNIYKQX.

**274** YP QSPBI UAP KCFQU UYPRZP

WVBUAQ VK VJF HACRIFPB'Q

RCZPQ UPGHACBE UAPW UV

YGRT GBI UGRT, GBI UAP BPMU

UYPRZP UPRRCBE UAPW UV QCU

IVYB GBI QAJU JS.

—SAXRRCQ ICRRPF

**275** ABZN JBFCA RTH'Y PTHKFN
KNRLALBH-ZTCLHX WNEM ONFF.
YTCN ZN, JBE LHAYTHRN: L
PTWN T IP.K. LH DHKNRFTENK.

**276** WVLZF LOZGJZ KZWFN HV
LCZFWUK TK UNKACBWLFBNL
NWBX NHTZLCBRE LCWL DFHYECL
LZWFN LH TK ZKZN: "RH CWDGH
BREGZN."

—FHRRBZ NCWIZN

**277** JXR QROVHP PWU VS W PBRJ
BQ WDCWUQ RWQBRF JXWH JXR
SBFQJ. ZU JXR QROVHP UVI'FR
VSS BJ.

—MWOEBR KDRWQVH

**278** PQ PSRXVF YSEVO IXMYOFVA.
HXV JSKYO XWEV BMEVA
WAQRXMAB MG M XWO DVVA
SAV.

—BFSKIXS PWFN

**279** JA VTERFMAJVD IXME UTMMBM
ERN NAIJK DVJMAVM CJDVRZMTD
W VNTM URT LXWI QJKKMC ERN,
WAC IXMA IXME TMZJZM ERN.
HNI LXWI JU ERN UTRBM IR
CMWIX?

—FMRTFM SJKKMT

**280** T EPH P WLV LZ CPXPILGT PGQ
XDBBEB MDPM EPTQ "XLLJ
MDLILNODRU." QTIBXMRU
NGQBIGBPMD HBIB MDB HLIQE
"JBBA ZILSBG." T XPG'M QL
WLMD.

**281** NO TQHIEGRF RWGUP QYIDR RWF
GURFEUFR GB RWQR OID PFR RI
PI GURI RWF AEGHQRF JIEKX IT
EFQK ZEFFAB JGRWIDR WQHGUP
RI BNFKK RWFN.

—AFUU VGKKFRRF

**282** WHQQRZLDD RD KIXT GLZJRDJ
JLCCRZN KIX RJ UIZ'J WXTJ HZG
JWLZ WHORZN WRS YHJYW WRD
WHZG RZ JWL GTRCC.

—AIWZZK YHTDIZ

**283** LB L PQX'C VEC, L HLGG PLV.
LB L'I PVEP, L TEX'C HQYO.
RQ HWS EYVX'C IS ZYQTVYLVR
E CEJ-PVPMTCLFGV FMRLXVRR
VJUVXRV?

**284** W ... BIDYDI JA VDD JCD FEIP
VWFD AY JCWTXV. JCD XQEVV
WV EQHESV CEQY DOBJS. ETF
ZIEZPDF. ETF W GRVJ ZRJ OS
QWB AT WJ. ETF ZCWBBDF E
JAAJC.

—GETDETD XEIAYEQA

**285** YZV QDEWVFAV ZJA KGNV YG
JD VDP ED ZGQAYGD, MZVFV
YZVFV'A J AYJFXQKTA JKFGAA
YZV AYFVVY BFGN J AYJFXQKTA.

—IVMEA XIJKT

**286** WIU HBJURWJYJB WIUSNL J
KJPU XUHW JH WIFW WIU NJRMH
SY HFWGNR FNU BSVCSHUT
URWJNUKL SY KSHW FJNKJRU
KGMMFMU.

—VFNP NGHHUKK

**287** CQJF VSP ZS LFXS ESPNX VSP

KNJ HPXXLFZ VSPN DKXJ LFXS

XQJ QKFUW SD XCJABJ HJSHAJ

CQS CJNJF'X WTKNX JFSPZQ XS

ZJX SPX SD YPNV UPXV.

—FSNT ENSWOV

**288** XJLOPICQ BZI NJB ZJT JMMIJLIQ

PE BZI OYEEH MJMILT TPENI BZI

CJBI TIWIEBPIT. JT J LITYCB,

ZI VJH SI ICPXPSCI BU LINIPWI

EPEI CPOIBPVI JNZPIWIVIEB

JGJLQT.

**289** SGAQO RDHQYJQ, AXSA

VXDJX JMCQR YQSOQRA

AM QLIOQRRDYN AXQ

DYQLIOQRRDKHQ DR CBRDJ.

—SHTMBR XBLHQE

**290** DBM XA JZAJGZ VHZ WBZ
ZYJIZHHUAR "RZZXGZHH
WA HFM" PZOAIZ HFMURS
HATZWBURS ZEZIMPAXM
FGIZFXM NRZD? UO MAV XAR'W
RZZX WA HFM UW, HBVW VJ.

**291** TSOJN NPK BYINYO NYUB AK
NPK VYYB LKGJ: S GEJ VYSLV NY
PEHK E BSJKEJK LEAKB ETNKO
AK.

—JNKHK AEONSL

**292** R EAZ'L AMZ X UAKNCLST. R'K
MXRLRZH JAT LVS YRZE MVSTS
R UXZ WAAY XL LVS GUTSSZ XZE
GXP "VSP, R ZSSE X NRBBX" XZE
AZS UAKSG ACL XZE VRLG KS RZ
LVS SPSQTAMG.

—YXLVWSSZ KXERHXZ

**293** PZ'W LIZ KMOEEQ OL OEE-QIG-
FOL-MOZ DGHHMZ PH QIG FOL
MOZ ZRPLXW ZROZ OKML'Z
IHHMKMA. PZ'W YGWZ O WITM-
IH-CROZ-QIG-FOL-MOZ DGHHMZ.

**294** CWXM T CSZ S VTK TM
XAXOXMBSUN ZHWPPA, BWX
BXSHWXU SZVXK OX BP KTZHDZZ
"OPJN-KTHV." ZP T ZSTK, "TB
ZBUTVXZ OX SZ S LADR QPU
BWX CWSATMR TMKDZBUN."

—YPWM SZBTM

**295** VKB RJYBFECBEV OQWO JESW
VKGFVW-VKFBB MBFXBEV JZ
QCBFGXQEO KQYB FBVLFEBP
VKBGF XBEOLO ZJFCO. KJN PJ
VKBW AEJN VKQV?

—XJSGE DLGEE

**296** ZXNP UXLHJQ KHZ NFKMOBZMLD
QBZNU LD VJLZXMDW UL IN RND
IMJJ TDLI IXND ZXNP WL LHZ LG
UZPJN.

—WBOOP UXBDQJMDW

**297** HQVO GLYEO L CKRAKAR QG
AGOLKA WAQH LG UKAGDE,
QGR APAG OEA JQLOAK JQV
VSKXKLVAR. LO JQV Q DELGAVA
KAVOQSKQGO.

—EAGGZ ZCSGYWQG

**298** PFYQWL MD ZNQK LFG
RPPMWQKURXXL BRXX FBB R
PXMBB RKW WMQ. UIREQWL MD
ZNQK M NRCQ R NRKEKRMX.

—YQX HIFFVD

**299** BP REVBCHD BU HNC UJBIC LP
YBPC, FEVVBETC BU HNC MBT
IEQ LP YCPHLRCV UJEF.

—ZLNQQD IEVULQ

**300** LMDKEQPBOQPZMDF—AMB GQTY
SBFP FMOTYC LEAWPMKEQI
DBIUYE PGEYY GBDCEYC. Z GQTY
DM KMMC EYQFMD PM IYDPZMD
PGZF.

**301** J UBP WO W JO ERJVBQBERK
AGMWLQG J EHBTGS PRWP NK
EHBIGQQBH SJSO'P GZJQP.

—FLSK PGOLPW

**302** CXWL ZMXCCJXMR CXGPLMC OCN
BXM IYFC XH VXJ IX ZXWFGLIL
O FQEEGL BOCILM. CYWFGD RX
JVOI Y RX — FQI OH Y YH LPLMD
CKQOML.

**303** RZV UVBKHW NUBWTYBUVWRK

BWT NUBWTEZQJTUVW NVR

BJHWN KH GVJJ QK RZBR RZVD

ZBLV B EHAAHW VWVAD.

—KBA JVLVWKHW

**304** P VNSBEPC LWXKPN EAGLLTGAK

YPL PJGWV GXD YWXKADK PXK

UGAVN PXLTDAL, IPNJD VDX GU

TYBEY EGISABLD VYD VYDID.

VYBXM PJGWV NGWA EGCCDOD

KPNL—BU NGW TAGVD P VDAI

SPSDA VYPV TPL XBXDVN-VYADD

SDAEDXV GUU-VGSBE, NGW'K

ODV PX U.

**305** Y LFPG CR TRXDPCP YJ FDRBCF,

HJG CSPJ Y BPHOYWPG: ERL THJ

VLE CBRDSYPF. JRQ Y'X IRRG HC

PNPBECSYJI.

—GPXPCBY XHBCYJ

**306** VG'C UTUEVBD GNUG GNH

UTXMBG XP BHFC GNUG

NUZZHBC VB GNH FXASW HYHAR

WUR USFURC OMCG HLUIGSR

PVGC GNH BHFCZUZHA.

          —OHAAR CHVBPHSW

**307** P VQJ IHSS P'B NHIIPJN RSGHC,

WHVQLFH P YPJG BZFHSY LFPJN

URCGF SPXH "FDQVPRLF,"

"CRRBZ," QJG "VRBYRCIQWSH"

UMHJ P'B WLZPJN LJGHCUHQC.

          —CHJR NRRGQSH

**308** D'UA ZAFDZAZ BL AYDVCYS HDJJ

NA "SA ZDZ AUAPLVSDKQ VSA

ZGFVGPX VGJZ SDB VG. DPGKDF,

CDK'V DV?"

**309** AG JRJQJGOPIK NFEBBR, AG

FPNJ BU UAIJ KBL EPYJ OB RAGJ

LZ CLAJORK AG P NAGMRJ UARJ

UIBQ NQPRRJNO OB RPIMJNO.

VEPO AN OEJ RBMAF? XB OPRR

ZJBZRJ SLIG NRBVJI?

—VPIIJG ELOFEJINBG

**310** FB FY NSTSJ'Y BVT YDS BUWY

YDUY YDS YR LSY UJI YDS

TSBTFXSTUYVT UTS LV BUT

UOUTY, LVGS VB PL NVPEIJ'Y

XSY UJM SHSTWFLS UY UEE.

—QVSM UIUGL

**311** MNNP KAWL: L IBTW

ONJJWOSKNY NC, ZLF, SQN

SINBZLYA NC SINZW VLRLYWZW

YBEMWH-THKA RBXXJWZ. OLJJ

KS "MWLBONBR ZBANPB."

**312** B YN OTGZJ VC Z TBIITG. BS
ONXCZJA BR ONXBJW, B'TT PBCG
IUG TBCRIBOL NSS IUG XBTL
ONJIZBJGD.

—GTZAJG FNNRTGD

**313** PU EDBKU D ULRSHLU ULPU
AZ GDEY VPK HRDTH PBRSTX
DT QDBQGYK. ULYT D HRU UR
GRRODTH QGRKYB, PTX DU'K
PQUSPGGZ P XRVTVPBX KIDBPG.

—URA BZPT

**314** FS CAGRBWQ BWQ U QUQW'M
GUIW B TNJWATMUBD
BINJJFJWM. LJ GUIWJQ B
FAMABD GAUVUQJ TBVM.

—NPGJBWWJ RBNN

**315** L DP OCG THMNBEO MQ D PLVGN
PDHHLDYG. PA QDOCGH ZDF D
PDW DWN PA PMOCGH ZDF D
ZMPDW.

**316** LROT J LDN D ZJX LO PDXO
PFTOW IW AFJTA BF BRO
RFKNON FY COFCHO LRF RDXT'B
NRFGOHOX BROJS NTFL,
NHJCCJTA, DTX NKJTA BROP.

—IJHH ISDKXJN

**317** GB GJ W FKLGPKJ UWFB
BXWB ZRPZER WLR VRHRL JP
BLGHGWE WJ NXRV BXRO BWQR
BXRSJREHRJ JRLGPKJEO.

—PJFWL NGEIR

**318** JS E AZMHZIK LTMVQ, MEA
DGWJI LTGVQ STK CEOZ KT KERZ
KCZ FVEDZ HTM PESP EIKJOJKX.
WYGEMZ QESIZ DGWJI LTGVQ.

**319** KBWLPDWLK DP PYQLK POVLL
RLBRSL PB FDR WL TR, JTP
BMAL Y XVLKK NLPK RYKP WH
ODRK, DP'K YSCYHK CBVPO DP.
—WYVDKKY ZYVLP CDMBQTV

**320** XQ LSYTOKZM BMSJZB VJIE KW
ZBM KFZMOFSZKTFSJ BTIWM
TL RSFVSCMW. EMVSIWM FT
XSZZMO NBSZ QTI NMKHB,
ZBMOM NKJJ SJNSQW EM
WTXMTFM NBT NMKHBW S
BIFAOMA SFA LKLZQ RTIFAW
XTOM ZBSF QTI.
—JMNKW EJSVC

**321** EWGNC ZXDCTU NKX JEX ACPR

LKXNJWKXU JENJ NPPAS JEXDK

LEDPMKXC JA LAGX ZNLF EAGX.

—ZDPP LAUZR

**322** EV E'T RSRF BYWNM ZD K

FRBOEFKYZF ZF K QEVR-

BWOOZFY BLBYRT, E

JRVEDEYRQL UKDY YZ CR

WDOQWXXRJ. CWY DZY WDYEQ

E'T JZUD YZ K BEAR REXIY.

—IRDFERYYR TKDYRQ

**323** GUPBAMQEKEBQ EM PB

LCVGEVBPI GECL. DLVDIL

GYPKLI GUVTMPBOM VR CEILM

GV WL ZEGU DLVDIL GULX VBIX

MLL VBFL P XLPY, PBO GULB

OEMFVKLY VBFL P XLPY EM ZPX

GVV VRGLB.

—HVUBBX FPYMVB

**324** R YDPV KN TDX D ADXL XLV

ZXLVM JDN.... LV VFUZNVJ RX,

RX BDQ CSF CZM KV. XLV CSM

BZSGJ QXRTW XZ KN XZFYSV,

ASX ZXLVM XLDF XLDX ...

—QXVPV KDMXRF


**325** F SFPP ZVJVO UEOAVB KT UFORB

WXT EU RHDEEP. KT KEK SECV

KV MG, AEB KV WOVRRVW, KXWV

KT YVW, XZW UVW KV. KXZ, WFW

BDV AMTR FZ BDV WEOK BVXRV

KV.

—KFHDXVP XOEZFZ


**326** ILV NBXIVCGVX BTJVG PV,

"OLBI'MM DAS LBQV?" F TBFG

"TSXKXFTV PV." LV TLAOVG PV B

CBJVG KFZISXV AW PD OFWV.

—XAGCVD GBCEVXWFVMG

**327** PTJH STJ PJYSTJD DJXGDS
OYVO STJDJ'O Y RQYOT RQGGC
PYDHFHE FH JRRJKS AHSFQ
HGGH, F YQPYVO PGHCJD TGP
STJ PYSJD WHGPO PTYS SFIJ SG
OSGX.

**328** YU MRGDW XB XKWH KRBW R
JWRXKWZ MKRUUWD, XJWUXH-
TYLZ KYLZV YT JWRXKWZ. JW
KRQ VYEWXKCUA DCIW XKRX
JKWZW C AZWJ LS. JW MRDDWQ
CX R JCUQYJ.

— QRU VSWUMWZ

**329** MNAWPHZ MB K HMC, K FMMV
PW QKJ'W FZWA BLPZJH. PJWPHZ
MB K HMC, PA'W AMM HKLV AM
LZKH.

— CLMNURM QKLE

**330** K HQPI YN IKWV LKG
MQCWVPQL. WVBW'L VCI
K TPBQSPU WC UBSDP ...
IBKWKSH XCQ WVP MBWVQCCJ.

—MCM VCNP

**331** VLNC JSC, "YMIJ KDI'V WATT
BNDBTN, BNDBTN WATT
BNDBTN." HMV A VLAIW VLN
YMIJ LNTB. OMJV JVSIKAIY
VLNZN JSCAIY "HSIY!" KDNJI'V
ZNSTTC LMZV SICHDKC.

—NKKAN APPSZK

**332** CMD GHQ ZNHUQ H ZMF PUMI
FKN WSJGMONUC GKHQQNZ.
PMU NRHIXZN, FKN BMUZW'J
ZHUYNJF KDIHQ LUNHJFJ,
DQNQKHQGNW LC JDUYNUC,
BNUN JSEN PMUFC-NSYKF-O.

**333** XF CQVGROPIODRV DRIKLRO

LIDRG XR. YLR SYRG DU WQVG

IVF REKSYR DU AQKC UV XR,

RYARKQITTF GSOQVP VIA DQXR.

TQCR Q'X DLR UVTF PSF NLU

YTRRAY VICRG.

—JOQIV CQTRF

**334** S WXDUDEN VKOZDCN DW

LVNGN OVNQ OSZR OK QKX

XCODZ QKX EKC'O YNNZ

ZDRN RDZZDCJ QKXGWNZY.

NFSUOZQ OVN KHHKWDON KY

ONZNBSGRNODCJ.

—ESCS WCKL

**335** KETOU JLSUAC OBL CLZLUNW

DLBQLUN MONLB, OUX MSNK

CRTL, NKL BLCN SC QRPPOALU.

—TOBNSU TEPP

**336** BJAXS JX VMZVVOT: Z
LVVTZFAVO WJUV JB WN HJJS
SLNU VJ L EJARYO JB ROJRYO
MZVQ GJJSJJ SJYYU ELXEOYZXH
OLEQ JVQOT JAV.

**337** HIPZZMPICZ GZN MPICZ UQJU
MN HPGDC AGU CPF'U. QJBN
OPG NBNI DPPYNC JU OPGI
MJUHQ JFC ZJSC, "RO XPZQ,
DPPY JU UQN USRN! S QJBN UP
QSN!"?

**338** A USD DX DOMT-QXLDQAXFD
CVSC UVOL A USD SC S
TXXCRSMM HSZO SLE CVO
IMSJOBD UOLC ALCX S VFEEMO,
A CVXFHVC CVOJ UOBO
CSMWALH SRXFC ZO.

— GSQWAO ZSDXL

**339** NFDJZ EFDQYIRZ GPIG DJZ BFZ'G

BF JZFCOP, TCG RG'M WFCX FNZ

HICYG. WFC GXIRZ WFCX DIZ GF

BF ZFGPRZO. WFC EIZ'G TYIDJ

MFDJFZJ HFX ZFG VZFNRZO NPIG

PRM FX PJX LFT MPFCYB TJ.

—LJZZRHJX IZRMGFZ

**340** NZJ SEZT TDCG AJFR HB?

YBZYIB TDZ RHZSB OUFCVR UE

VBRGCJVCEGR. GDCG'R TDN U

CITCNR OCVVN C TCGBV YURGZI

XUIIBM TUGD FCRZIUEB.

—YCJI YVZLBEKC

**341** YN CXJKAVI BSBA'V ZLGK YK.

VDKN OJLAEKB YN OXON IDLKI

FSVD YN TKKV IVSZZ SA VDKY.

—FLLBN XZZKA

**342** YHEQ ZGBOEQSHE ... O MHUC SI

DOK H FF MVW. GC MHUC SC H

ENCHQEGOBQ NOQG H

FVYY'E-CIC PW QGC FHZD.

—BPKWCI KHWMCBROCYK

**343** CZO XOBQ A RYBXOV YAKKYO

YOBMIO EBGOEBYY BZV WX

VBV NBG KFO HCBHF. FBYPNBX

KFQCIMF KFO GOBGCZ FO

KQBVOV WO KC BZCKFOQ

PBWAYX.

—VBLAV HCQQBVC

**344** R GRYW HCU IKHG-KIVKKO

RYJCODZKEKYIRAHK. UEF EBVK

FCQZIKHG, UEKY FCQ JBY EBVK

CVEKZI?

—BOF BIEVCY

**345** K'WG HYZBMYH JTZBH YJWKCM J
QJRKXU. K SBFH YJWGC'H FGGC
JCU HYJH PGJXXU JDDGJX HZ RG.

—XJBPJ NKMYHXKCMGP

**346** DAL NLP UO TUWADULJ DAVP
DAL OZXJQ VPQ YXPOUQLJVSKM
LVOULJ DX ZJUDL ZUDA.

—TVJDM RLKQTVP

**347** BKKDQGWT IEBI YGIEYS IEY
AYLI ZGWT MS IEY SGTEI ZGWT
TBGWYU RMWISMA ML IEY
RMDWISH, GI ZMDAU NSMPBPAH
LAH BSMDWU GW RGSRAYK.

—NBI NBDAKYW

**348** H AXF'O IZMY CYO CYYMYD
QHPY DXKY CYXCQY. H IZMY
JIXQY PYFFYQD XV HUUHOZOHXF.

—JIXXCH BXQANYUB

**349** OJG MFGF TA OTZQIIT QVGP'O

TZXSTMF VSLJO TAA OJG ZQO.

DTM FJVGN SO MR, RMO SO TP

Q RSGIG TA RQRGV, VTEE SO MR

QPN FOSIY SO ZGOKGGP DTMV

ESRF ... QPN FGO ASVG OT SO.

— ZTZ PGKJQVO

**350** JW YJLZRG BG PGGF WEZGMZXR.

IJL PGQGZ DPJB BCGP RJXG PLS

ER AJEPA SJ YJXG LU SJ IJL MPF

RMI RJXGSCEPA HEDG, "IJL'ZG

WEZGF." IJL AJSSM VG ZGMFI.

— FMQG MSSGHH

**351** KI NHXVGVH KW IHNBBNTHD,

OGA YVP'E LDVLHD OGV YFKPM

NPY WBVMD CJWE TJFWE KPEV

IHNBDW?

**352** P WVSPJEPD FPD VYJHVDYQ P

TSSC JS BEM ISWPI IETVPVK

NSVJK KYPVM PNJYV TSVVSXEDZ

EJ, QHVEDZ XBEWB JEFY BY

DYOYV ZSJ PVSHDQ JS VYPQEDZ

EJ.


**353** PBRJ S PNF NWICD DRJ PR

UIHRV WRONCFR UM KNDBRL

FIYV ICL BICFR. FIURBIP DBR

YNJVYILV KICJV ICD NWICD SD,

NJV PR BNV DI TI.

—N. PBSDJRM WLIPJ


**354** LWCI RIE PAMKJ JG JAXLJQLK FLJ

ZL DAFFAT JQL PRKLLKW AD RFF

ZS DRGAKVJL RJQFLJLW.

—ULDD WJVFWAI

**355** CM GIF FTFR VKF GIF DCOZXDR
GX GIF RXYN, GIFO DIT ZXFR CG
IYKG DIFO C RLKVT GIFQ DCGI
DCOZFJ?

—RGFLIFO WXNAFKG

**356** XEEAHUGYV LA OAUBHY
XKLHAYAOBHK, KWXEB GK
SGYGLB. LIGK GK X FBHD
EAOSAHLGYV LIAQVIL,
WXHLGEQRXHRD SAH WBAWRB
TIA EXYYAL HBOBONBH TIBHB
LIBD RBSL LIGYVK.

—TAAUD XRRBY

**357** GPK NQYZ GPTQA GN UN XTGP
HLETYZ DVKYKGNQD TD GN GLVK
GPKE NIG NH GPK JYNDKG LQU
ULQJK XTGP GPKE.

—LIGPNB IQVQNXQ

**358** F TBID GEZGDEMQ FJ NZO

BJVDNDO. B TZMDN FO TZNSFJV

MYZ ZC PQ OHFMABODO.

—OZHGQ OBNDO

**359** WG W CZJIQD N EJTZRJ

CZZR, WD SZJVT KHNU DQH

DHAAZAWEDE QNMH SZU.

—NKHAWPNU PAZEESZAT YJBBVH

DZJAUNKHUD AHIJVNA

HVVHU AWYEDHWU

**360** ZBJYITKSPTKRBJQ ... RE

DBS EBSJV KGW QWZIWK

UWQQTYW GRVVWJ RJ KGWQW

ZIDFKBYITUQ, DBS URYGK NW T

ZBJQFRITZD KGWBIRQK.

# ANSWERS

**1** Fun thing to do on a really dull Sunday afternoon: Try solving the New York Times crossword using only pieces of "Magnetic Poetry."

**2** Message from a recent fortune cookie: "No one is ever too old to learn, but many people keep putting it off anyway."

**3** Always forgive your enemies; nothing annoys them so much.

—Oscar Wilde

**4** It's amazing how much work I could have done in the time I've spent waiting for my computer to start.

**5** Physician: Someone to whom you give exorbitant amounts of money to tell you things you were happier not knowing.

**6** Organized crime in America takes in over forty billion dollars a year and spends very little on office supplies.

—Woody Allen

**7** You know there is a problem with the education system when you realize that out of the three R's, only one begins with R.

—Dennis Miller

**8** It took me seventeen years to get three thousand hits in baseball. I did it in one afternoon on the golf course.

—Hank Aaron

**9** I have low self-esteem. When we were in bed together, I would fantasize that I was someone else.

—Richard Lewis

**10** We're told to live every day as if it were our last. So today I have an appointment to be autopsied.

**11** Seize the moment. Remember all those women on the Titanic who waved off the dessert cart.

—Erma Bombeck

**12** I told my psychiatrist that everyone hates me. He said I was being ridiculous; everyone hasn't met me yet.

—Rodney Dangerfield

**13** A new study reveals U.S. students have very little knowledge of American history. In fact, test scores are the lowest since the Lincoln-Nixon debates.

—Conan O'Brien

**14** TV has changed.... Immediacy is the key. With everyone Twittering now, information is only good for about a day.

—Jay Leno

**15** The pig is an amazing animal. If you feed a pig an apple, it makes bacon. I find that impressive.

—Jim Gaffigan

**16** There's so much plastic in this culture that vinyl leopard skin is becoming an endangered synthetic.

—Lily Tomlin

**17** A bookstore is one of the only pieces of evidence we have that people are still thinking.

—Jerry Seinfeld

**18** It's important to remember that apparently, by elimination, dishonesty is the second-best policy.

—George Carlin

**19** I don't like the idea that people can call you in your car. I think there's news you shouldn't get at sixty miles an hour.

—Tom Parks

**20** All these TV reality shows make me wonder ... Is there anyone, anywhere, whom absolutely nobody thinks needs a makeover?

**21** Certain tribes in Borneo do not have a word for "no" and consequently turn down requests by nodding their heads and saying "I'll get back to you."

—Woody Allen

**22** Fall is my favorite season in Los Angeles, watching the birds change color and fall from the trees.

—David Letterman

**23** There are patriotic vegetarians in the American Legion who will only eat animals that were killed in combat.

—George Carlin

**24** He was cheating on me with his secretary. I found lipstick on his collar, covered with Wite-Out.

—Wendy Liebman

**25** There was an item in the paper today: A lion got loose in the Central Park Zoo in New York, and was severely mauled.

—Bob Newhart

**26** Marriage is real tough because you have to deal with feelings, and lawyers.

—Richard Pryor

**27** I wanted to buy a candle holder but the store didn't have one, so I got a cake.

—Mitch Hedberg

**28** A black cat crossing your path signifies that the animal is going somewhere.

—Groucho Marx

**29** Zooming gas prices have everyone stunned.... People in L.A. may seriously start thinking about walking the two blocks to the store.

—Jay Leno

**30** Blood may be thicker than water, but it is still sticky, unpleasant, and generally nauseating

—Janeane Garofalo

**31** All the problems we face in the United States today can be traced to an unenlightened immigration policy on the part of the American Indian.

—Pat Paulsen

**32** Reputation is an idle and most false imposition, oft got without merit and lost without deserving.

—William Shakespeare

**33** There's debate now on whether pilots should carry guns. On the one hand, the skies would be safer. On the other hand, guns and alcohol don't mix.

—Conan O'Brien

**34** I don't expect anyone to agree with all my votes. I don't agree with all of them myself.

—Arlen Specter

**35** A petting zoo is a great place, if you want your kid's clothes to end up inside a goat's stomach.

—Bil Dwyer

**36** The record for highest-scoring single play in a Scrabble game is three hundred sixty-five points. The word was "quixotry."

**37** So what if I don't have "abs of steel"? Isn't it good enough that I have a cast-iron stomach?

**38** When you're in love, it's the most glorious two and a half days of your life.

—Richard Lewis

**39** If it's the Psychic Network, why do they need a phone number?

—Robin Williams

**40** Leather jackets scare me. Think about it, people are ... spending five hundred dollars to wear beef jerky.

—Brad Stine

**41** Worried that the phrase might be removed from U.S. money, a Chicago school bus driver petitioned to legally change his name to "In God We Trust."

**42** April is National Poetry Month ... which is silly, because nothing rhymes with "April" or "month." Shouldn't it be a day in May? Or a June afternoon?

**43** People who don't eat enough carbs might be skinny, but aren't they always cranky?

—Rachael Ray

**44** Maybe one reason the current First Family named their puppy Bo is that "Obama Bo" is a palindrome? Nah, probably not.

**45** It's true: A woman from Norfolk, England, recently learned she had been celebrating her birthday one day late for over a century.

**46** Shame is an unhappy emotion invented by pietists in order to exploit the human race.

—from the screenplay "Victor/Victoria"

**47** Lead us not into temptation. Just tell us where it is; we'll find it.

—Sam Levenson

**48** I count myself in nothing else so happy / As in a soul remembering my good friends.

—Shakespeare, "Richard II"

**49** The secret to flying is to throw yourself at the ground and miss.

—from "The Hitchhiker's Guide to the Galaxy"

**50** Chuck Barris, explaining how easy it was to create "Newlywed Game": "All I needed was four couples, eight questions, and a washer-dryer."

**51** The metric system did not really catch on in the States, unless you count the increasing popularity of the nine-millimeter bullet.

—Dave Barry

**52** When my wife asked me to start a garden, the first thing I dug up was an excuse.

—Henny Youngman

**53** My old boyfriend used to say, "I read Playboy for the articles." Right, and I go to shopping malls for the music.

—Rita Rudner

**54** Odd fact: Bolivia has a naval force with thousands of sailors and over one hundred fifty boats, despite being a landlocked nation.

**55** A snail can travel over a razor blade without cutting itself. Or to put it another way, scientists get bored.

—Jimmy Carr

**56** Red meat is not bad for you. Now, blue-green meat ... that's bad for you.

—Tommy Smothers

**57** A regular customer at my local diner complained when the prices went up. I told him it was because they had to offset the cost of printing menus with the new prices on them.

**58** Marriage is like a five-thousand-piece jigsaw puzzle, all sky.

—Cathy Ladman

**59** Thirty-six prisoners escaped from a jail in the African nation of Guinea by digging through a wall with spoons.

**60** I have never watched "American Idol," but I'm thankful we're living in a country where we can actually afford to waste your time.

—Arlo Guthrie

**61** On the back of a NyQuil bottle it says "May cause drowsiness." It should say "Don't make any plans."

—Denis Leary

**62** Anyone can be a golf announcer. All you have to do is use that voice you use when you call in sick at work.

—Mike Rowe

**63** Someone might tell you that marriage is just a piece of paper. Well, so is money, and what's more life-affirming than cold, hard cash?

—Dennis Miller

**64** Ever since nineteen-twenty-nine, the citizens of Burlington, Wisconsin, have held an annual contest to determine who their biggest liar is.

**65** Suburbia is where the developer bulldozes out the trees, then names the streets after them.

—Bill Vaughan

**66** "Logophobia" is defined as "a fear of words." But if you have a fear of words, how do you tell the psychiatrist? The moment he asks "What's the problem?" you'll run screaming!

**67** If I was paid a dollar for every time my dad said he loved me.... Well, money isn't important now.

—Larry the Cable Guy

**68** The older I get, the simpler the definition of maturity seems: It's the length of time between when I realize someone is a jackass and when I tell them that they're one.

—Brett Butler

**69** The technological advance I wish I could get is an addition to my answering machine: a get-to-the-point button.

—Alicia Brandt

**70** There is no idea so patently absurd that it can't catch on.

—Bill Maher

**71** Welcome to New York, where every tourist is a walking ATM machine.

—David Letterman

**72** I think I am a pretty good judge of people, which is why I hate most of them.

—Roseanne Barr

**73** I've killed so many plants. I walked into a nursery once, and my face was on a wanted poster.

—Rita Rudner

**74** I had general anesthesia.... You go to sleep in one room, and then wake up four hours later in a totally different room. Just like college.

—Ross Shafer

**75** Nothing ends a comedian's career faster than regular sex and being in love.

—Patton Oswalt

**76** A Florida woman was recently arrested for driving around a store parking lot with her three-year-old granddaughter sitting on the roof of the automobile.

**77** If I wasn't waylaid by early childhood stardom, I would have become an engineer or a scientist.

—Christopher Knight, alias TV's Peter Brady

**78** Two Americans have won the Nobel Prize in economics. They're the first to figure out all of the little charges on their phone bill.

—Jay Leno

**79** The moment a child begins resenting his parents coincides with the moment the parents determine the child is now too heavy to carry anymore.

**80** Why does the Air Force need expensive new bombers? Have the people we've been bombing over the years been complaining?

—George Wallace

**81** I write a book for no other reason than to add three or four hundred acres to my magnificent estate.

—Jack London

**82** I'm kind of paranoid.... I often think the car in front of me is following me the long way around.

—Dennis Miller

**83** Why is it that, more often than not, the person who exuberantly yells "That's what I'm talkin' about!" hadn't said anything to that point?

**84** I'd like to have kids. I get those maternal feelings. Like when I'm lying on the couch and I can't reach the remote control.

—Kathleen Madigan

**85** Census workers have been attacked by people they're trying to interview. No one knows how many.

—Jon Stewart

**86** I admit it; I'm a hypochondriac. But I manage to control it with a placebo.

—Dennis Miller

**87** When it says "six to twelve pounds" on the side of the Pampers box, they're not lying. That is all those things will hold.

—Jeff Foxworthy

**88** The shoulder surgery was a success. The lobotomy failed.
—coach Mike Ditka, on quarterback
Jim McMahon's operation

**89** Today I saw a red-and-yellow sunset and thought how insignificant I am. Of course, I thought that yesterday too, and it rained.

—Woody Allen

**90** When a TV crime show advertises with the phrase "ripped from the headlines," doesn't that just mean the writers couldn't come up with anything original?

**91** When Hamlet yelled at Ophelia to "Get thee to a nunnery!" he may have been using an Elizabethan slang word for "brothel."

**92** Happiness is having a large, loving, caring, close-knit family in another city.

—George Burns

**93** Just last week some guy pulled a knife on me. I could see it wasn't a real professional job. There was butter on it.

—Rodney Dangerfield

**94** I've put in so many enigmas and puzzles that it will keep the professors busy for centuries arguing over what I meant.

—James Joyce

**95** Having been self-employed for well over twenty years now, I hold the record for consecutive "Employee of the Month" awards.

**96** I get plenty of exercise carrying the coffins of my friends who exercise.

—Red Skelton

**97** If God didn't want us to eat meat, He would have made cows run faster.

—Aisha Tyler

**98** My friend has a severe case of hypochondria. He thinks he's dead.

—Craig Sharf

**99** We sleep in separate rooms, we have dinner apart, we take separate vacations. We're doing everything we can to keep our marriage together.

—Rodney Dangerfield

**100** Cryptogram haiku
created for one purpose:
Empty space to fill.

**101** It has been my observation that if you take a carburetor apart and put it together again enough times, you will eventually have two of them.

—from a letter sent to the "Car Talk" guys

**102** We are all born charming, fresh, and spontaneous, and must be civilized before we are fit to participate in society.

—Judith "Miss Manners" Martin

**103** I come from a typical American family. Me, my mother, her third husband, his daughter from a second marriage, my stepsister, her illegitimate son.

—Carol Henry

**104** Some guy hit my fender, and I told him, "Be fruitful and multiply." But not in those words.

—Woody Allen

**105** I went to the thirtieth reunion of my preschool. I didn't want to go because I've put on, like, one hundred pounds.

—Wendy Liebman

**106** When you are about thirty-five years old, something terrible always happens to music.

—Steve Race

**107** Always end the name of your child with a vowel, so that when you yell the name will carry.

—Bill Cosby

**108** The no-killing commandment came after Abel was slain. Was Cain punished for committing an act that wasn't yet illegal?

**109** Coyotes are just like my relatives. They go out in pairs, they whine at night, and they go anywhere there's food.

—Billy Crystal

**110** The ad in the paper said "Big Sale! Last Week!" Why advertise? I already missed it. They're just rubbing it in.

—Yakov Smirnoff

**111** Nietzsche says that we will live the same life, over and over again. God, I'll have to sit through the Ice Capades again.

—Woody Allen

**112** The Japanese have developed an automated dog-washing machine. It's bad when you unload it and find an extra paw that doesn't match.

—Craig Kilborn

**113** If you know the average person is stupid, then realize that half are stupider than that.

—George Carlin

**114** I find it rather easy to portray a businessman. Being bland, rather cruel, and incompetent comes naturally to me.

—John Cleese

**115** When a group of people go into a restaurant and the maitre d' asks "How many are you?" I wonder if multiple personalities figure into the equation.

**116** On my sixteenth birthday my parents tried to surprise me with a car, but they missed.

—Tom Cotter

**117** The dentist told me I grind my teeth at night, so now before I go to sleep I fill my mouth with hot water and coffee beans.

—Jeff Marder

**118** I wasn't a very good accountant. I always felt that if you got within two or three bucks of it, that was close enough.

—Bob Newhart

**119** Buy thermometers in the wintertime. They're much lower then.

—Soupy Sales

**120** I have the body of an eighteen-year-old. I keep it in the fridge.

—Spike Milligan

**121** State legislators are merely politicians whose darkest secret prohibits them from running for higher office.

—Dennis Miller

**122** I went on a diet, swore off drinking and heavy eating, and in fourteen days I lost two weeks.

—Joe E. Lewis

**123** When I was little Mom would make chocolate frosting, and she'd let me lick the beaters. And then she'd turn them off.

—Marty Cohen

**124** You know you're getting old when you stoop to tie your shoelaces and wonder what else you could do while you're down there.

—George Burns

**125** Back in the fourteen-hundreds, people used to walk around going, "This is a long time ago."

—Gilbert Gottfried

**126** Most people don't know what they're doing. And a lot of them are really good at it.

—George Carlin

**127** The problem with cats is that they get the same exact look whether they see a moth or an ax murderer.

—Paula Poundstone

**128** Behind every failure is an opportunity somebody wishes they had missed.

—Lily Tomlin

**129** No matter how much the boss likes you, if you work in a bank you can't take home samples.

—Eddie Cantor

**130** 'Tis not enough to help the feeble up, But to support him after.

—Shakespeare, "Timon of Athens"

**131** During the interview portion of an episode of a popular TV game show, a contestant described herself as a "stay-at-home mom." Clearly, she was lying.

**132** Horse sense is the thing a horse has which keeps it from betting on people.

—W.C. Fields

**133** I'm the kind of guy who will have nothing all my life, and then they'll discover oil while they're digging my grave.

—George Gobel

**134** What's great about aspirin is that no matter how long you suck on it, it never loses its flavor.

—Gregg Rogell

**135** A friend of mine gave me a Philip Glass CD. I listened to it for five hours before I realized it had a scratch on it.

—Emo Philips

**136** I don't plan to grow old gracefully. I plan to have facelifts until my ears meet.

—Rita Rudner

**137** There's always one teacher you had a crush on. For me it's my wife's aerobics instructor.

—Brian Kiley

**138** Health nuts are going to feel stupid someday, lying in hospitals dying of nothing.

—Redd Foxx

**139** I once saw a headline about a new book by a local author, purporting to be a survival guide for the end of the world. What I'd like to know is, if the world ends, where will the survivors be?

**140** If you can remember to take ginkgo biloba every day, you don't need it.

—Ellen DeGeneres

**141** I sold my house this week. I got a pretty good price for it, but it made my landlord mad as hell.

—Garry Shandling

**142** I just saw my grandmother, probably for the last time. She's not sick or anything, she just bores the hell out of me.

—A. Whitney Brown

**143** Always be nice to your children, because they are the ones who will choose your rest home.

—Phyllis Diller

**144** Little kids in a supermarket buy cereal the way men buy lingerie. They get stuff they have no interest in just to get the prize inside.

—Jeff Foxworthy

**145** All creatures must learn to coexist. That's why the brown bear and the field mouse can ... live in harmony. Of course they can't mate, or the mice would explode.

—Betty White

**146** Any sufficiently advanced technology is indistinguishable from magic.

—Arthur C. Clarke

**147** An economist is an expert who will know tomorrow why the things he predicted yesterday didn't happen today.

—Evan Esar

**148** My mom ... wakes me at six in the morning and says, "The early bird catches the worm." If I want a worm, ... I'll drink a bottle of tequila.

—Pam Stone

**149** Radio is a medium of entertainment which permits millions of people to listen to the same joke at the same time, and yet remain lonesome.

—T.S. Eliot

**150** In the original movie, the Invisible Man must be naked to stay unseen ... but as he runs through the snow, he leaves shoeprints.

**151** One afternoon I noticed a church's stained glass window and, the way the sunlight hit it, I would've sworn it looked just like a grilled cheese sandwich.

**152** Dogs feel very strongly that they should always go with you in the car, in case the need should arise for them to bark violently at nothing right in your ear.

—Dave Barry

**153** Getting married is a lot like getting into a tub of hot water. After you get used to it, it ain't so hot.

—Minnie Pearl

**154** Only in America do we shop at places with limited parking, overpriced items, and long lines and call them convenience stores.

—Yakov Smirnoff

**155** Size isn't everything. The whale is endangered, while the ant continues to do just fine.

—Bill Vaughan

**156** I need my sleep. I make no bones about it. I need eight hours a day, and at least ten at night.

—Bill Hicks

**157** You can always depend on the American people to do the right thing—once they've explored all the other possibilities.

—Winston Churchill

**158** I am as frustrated with society as a pyromaniac in a petrified forest.

—A. Whitney Brown

**159** My wife is an earth sign; I'm a water sign. Together we make mud.

—Rodney Dangerfield

**160** I'm taking remedial math so I can help my son make it to the third grade.

—Sinbad

**161** A cement mixer collided with a prison van. Motorists are asked to be on the lookout for sixteen hardened criminals.

—Ronnie Corbett

**162** I can't think of anything more horrible than sharing what I'm doing all day.

—Renee Zellweger, re Twitter

**163** Maybe hell is just having to listen to our grandparents breathe through their noses when they're eating sandwiches.

—Jim Carrey

**164** Those that would give up essential liberty to gain a little temporary safety deserve neither.

—Benjamin Franklin

**165** When you have sex your body emits a hormone that drifts down the hall into your child's room and makes them want a drink of water.

—Jeff Foxworthy

**166** I hate small towns because once you've seen the cannon in the park there's nothing else to do.

—Lenny Bruce

**167** Someone asked me, "What's your idea of a good time?" I said, "Six forty-five."

—Dick Cavett

**168** At thirty-three miles, the longest main street in the United States is in Island Park, Idaho.

**169** Never keep up with the Joneses. Drag them down to your level; it's cheaper.

—Quentin Crisp

**170** When daylight saving time starts, radio and TV announcers advise us that we will lose an hour of sleep. I don't. I lose an hour of doing stuff.

**171** I'm getting very comfortable with my body. I'm sleeping on a full-length mirror.

—Sandra Bernhard

**172** Sometimes I wonder whether the world is being run by smart people who are putting us on or by imbeciles who really mean it.

—Mark Twain

**173** A child of one can be taught not to do certain things, such as touch a hot stove, pull lamps off of tables, and wake Mommy before noon.

—Joan Rivers

**174** The best way to lose weight is to close your mouth, something very difficult for a politician.

—Ed Koch

**175** Having a child is surely the most beautiful irrational act that two people in love can commit.

—Bill Cosby

**176** Football combines the two worst features of American life: violence and committee meetings.

—George Will

**177** The drawback of a journey that has been too well planned is that it does not leave enough room for adventure.

—André Gide

**178** My parents were intelligent, enlightened people. They accepted me for what I was: a punishment from God.

—David Steinberg

**179** Cats instinctively know the precise moment their owners will awaken, and then they wake them ten minutes sooner.

—Jim Davis

**180** If a sheep can't fall asleep, what does it count? And how can fish sleep so peacefully with all those dead mobsters around?

**181** All you need is ignorance and confidence, and then success is assured.

—Mark Twain

**182** I arise in the morning torn between the desire to improve the world and a desire to enjoy the world. This makes it hard to plan the day.

—E.B. White

**183** I used to want to be a country-western singer, but I took a test and I had too much self-esteem.

—Brett Butler

**184** There comes a time when you should stop expecting other people to make a big deal about your birthday. That time is age eleven.

—Dave Barry

**185** You can tell it's the Christmas season. Stores are selling off their expired milk as eggnog.

—David Letterman

**186** The problem with fiction is that it must seem credible, while reality seldom is.

—Isabel Allende

**187** William Hopper (actor who played Perry Mason's P.I. aide on TV) is an anagram of Philip Marlowe (fictional sleuth in Raymond Chandler's novels).

**188** Reading made Don Quixote a gentleman. Believing what he read made him mad.

—George Bernard Shaw

**189** Home is the place where, when you have to go there, they have to take you in.

—Robert Frost

**190** When I see a mom carrying her young child in one of those wearable "baby harnesses" I think, "Wasn't nine months enough already?"

**191** The IRS is auditing the NRA. I haven't had this much trouble picking sides since the Iran-Iraq war.

—Bill Maher

**192** There ought to be an FAA requirement that crying babies have to go into the overhead compartment.

—Bobby Slayton

**193** They say if you watch fish, it helps you relax, to fall asleep. Which explains why I always doze off when I'm snorkeling.

—Ellen DeGeneres

**194** Don't go to a school reunion. There'll be a lot of old people there claiming to be your classmates.

—Tom Dreesen

**195** I buy books on suicide at bookstores. You can't get them at the library, because people don't return them.

—Kevin Nealon

**196** Many online businesses have closed, but the Internet still offers abundant options to discriminating shoppers, as long as what they want is porn.

—Vance DeGeneres

**197** I was getting C-SPAN and the Home Shopping Network on the same station. I actually bought a congressman.

—Bruce Baum

**198** If you ever want to torture my dad, tie him up and right in front of him, refold a road map incorrectly.

—Cathy Ladman

**199** What if everything is an illusion and nothing exists? In that case, I definitely overpaid for my carpet.

—Woody Allen

**200** I don't see the point of testing cosmetics on rabbits, because they're already cute.

—Rich Hall

**201** If it weren't for electricity we'd all be watching television by candlelight.

—George Gobel

**202** I don't even acknowledge Earth Day. I find it exceedingly jingoistic and quite unfair to the other planets.

**203** I'm chunky. In a bathing suit I look like a Bartlett pear with a rubber band around it.

—Drew Carey

**204** I don't believe for a second that weightlifting is a sport. They pick up a heavy thing and put it down again. To me, that's indecision.

—Paula Poundstone

**205** My ex-girlfriend ... reminded me of the Sphinx because she was very mysterious and eternal and solid, and her nose was shot off by French soldiers.

—Emo Philips

**206** In Seattle you haven't had enough coffee until you can thread a sewing machine while it's running.

—Jeff Bezos

**207** I used to go fishing until one day it struck me: You can buy fish. What the hell am I doing in a boat at four-thirty in the morning?

—Kenny Rogerson

**208** I saw a sign in a jewelry store window, "Ears Pierced While You Wait." The alternative staggers the imagination.

—Emily Levine

**209** When the government sets up a program designed to create thousands of jobs, it never involves skills I have. Where's the Federal Council for Bad Joke Writing?

**210** People keep telling us "There is no I in 'team.'" But you can snap the top piece off the T and make one.

**211** I wonder why women wear evening gowns to nightclubs. Why don't they wear nightgowns?

—George Carlin

**212** If you had a penny and threw it off the Empire State Building and it hit somebody in the head, it would kill him. Talk about getting your money's worth.

—Heywood Banks

**213** I don't have anything against facelifts, but I think it's time to stop when you look permanently frightened.

—Susan Norfleet

**214** My nephew ... was wearing a helmet, shoulder pads, kneepads, gloves, and saying, "I'm gonna ride my bike." Where? Through a minefield?

—Wanda Sykes

**215** I put a new engine in my car but didn't take the old one out. Now my car goes five hundred miles an hour.

—Steven Wright

**216** At a job interview, tell them you're willing to give a hundred and ten percent. Unless the job is statistician.

—Adam Gropman

**217** It is truly a shame when your seven-year-old son says, "Daddy, will you check my math?" and you have to lie and say, "I trust you, son."

—Sinbad

**218** Too bad the only people who know how to run the country are busy driving cabs and cutting hair.

—George Burns

**219** Why is the lavatory in a public building called the "restroom"? Does anybody go in there just to take a rest?

**220** A New Age store in my neighborhood had a display in the window, labeled "essential oils." I looked them over and decided, "No, they're not—I can do without them."

**221** The most important thing I learned from watching [the TV show "Cops"] is, the one way to avoid being arrested is to wear a shirt.

—Dennis Regan

**222** There's no such thing as fun for the whole family. There are no massage parlors with ice cream and free jewelry.

—Jerry Seinfeld

**223** God created humans on the sixth day and rested on the seventh. This explains a lot. How good is your output at the end of the workweek?

**224** Any man who can drive safely while kissing a pretty girl is simply not giving the kiss the attention it deserves.

—Albert Einstein

**225** What if it was cats who invented technology? Would they have TV shows starring rubber squeak toys?

—Douglas Coupland

**226** I'm willing to see prayer in our schools, if you're willing to find a place for algebra in our churches.

—Dylan Brody

**227** We never talked, my family. We communicated by putting Ann Landers articles on the refrigerator.

—Judy Gold

**228** I went to play golf and tried to shoot my age, but I shot my weight instead.

—Bob Hope

**229** My autobiography consists of five hundred blank pages. It's called "Me: The Untold Story."

**230** ... I was asked to redo my autobiography as a Broadway musical. I got so excited I couldn't compose myself.

**231** If creationists and evolutionists both took a good hard look at a platypus, they'd agree there must be a third explanation.

**232** What is the difference between a taxidermist and a tax collector? The taxidermist takes only your skin.

—Mark Twain

**233** Underground nuclear testing, defoliation of the rain forests, toxic waste ... if the world were a big apartment, we wouldn't get our deposit back.

—John Ross

**234** I called the Psychic Friends hotline. We spoke for six hours, and she didn't realize that I wasn't going to pay my bill.

—Michael Aronin

**235** A Democrat sees the glass of water as half-full; a Republican ... wonders who the hell drank half his glass of water.

—Jeff Cesario

**236** My favorite T-shirt slogan: "Why should I say excuse me when YOU were the one blocking the way?" It's printed on the back so people can read it after I shove them aside.

**237** Computers are invading our whole society. I just saw a tattoo parlor advertising that it has spell-check.

—Jay Leno

**238** People die of "natural causes," plural. Do they always work in tandem? Are they individually insufficient to kill?

**239** My wife thinks I'm too nosy. At least that's what she keeps writing in her diary.

—Drake Sather

**240** Why does a TV news report about a criminal at large always describe what witnesses saw him wearing? I bet he's had plenty of time to change by then.

**241** If you don't believe that America is anti-intellectual, then why is it that on "Gilligan's Island" the character who had the worst billing was the Professor?

—Bill Maher

**242** The problem with unemployment is that the minute you wake up in the morning, you're on the job.

—Slappy White

**243** A Chinese restaurant in my neighborhood had an item on their specials menu called "Vegetarian Chicken." How does that work, exactly?

**244** I don't like country music, but I don't mean to denigrate those who do. And for the people who like country music, denigrate means "put down."

—Bob Newhart

**245** Reader, suppose you were an idiot. And suppose you were a member of Congress. But I repeat myself.

—Mark Twain

**246** I was raised by just my mom. My father died when I was eight years old. At least, that's what he told us in the letter.

—Drew Carey

**247** You have to remember one thing about the will of the people: It wasn't that long ago that we were swept away by the Macarena.

—Jon Stewart

**248** A person is a success if he gets up in the morning and gets to bed at night and in between does what he wants to do.

—Bob Dylan

**249** The most blatant example of cruelty to animals is the rotisserie. It's just a really morbid Ferris wheel for chickens.

—Mitch Hedberg

**250** Some see a dark cloud and look for the silver lining. When they do, I remind them that silver tarnishes.

**251** If God doesn't destroy Hollywood Boulevard, He owes Sodom and Gomorrah an apology.

—Jay Leno

**252** A study of economics usually reveals that the best time to buy anything is last year.

—Marty Allen

**253** My parents ... live in a retirement community, which is basically a minimum-security prison with a golf course.

—Joel Warshaw

**254** I went snowboarding today. Well, actually I went careening off a mountain on a giant tongue depressor.

—Paul Provenza

**255** I took a two-year-old computer in to be repaired, and the guy looked at me as though he was a gun dealer and I'd brought him a musket.

—Jon Stewart

**256** We may not be able to imagine how our lives could be more frustrating and complex, but Congress can.

—Cullen Hightower

**257** I go through the refrigerator so many times at night my neighbors think we have a strobe light in the kitchen.

—Max Alexander

**258** Why are those flat, oblong candies called Mounds, when it's the Almond Joys that have mounds in them?

**259** I understand the inventor of the bagpipes was inspired when he saw a man carrying an indignant, asthmatic pig under his arm.

—Alfred Hitchcock

**260** The purpose of baseball is to stand in one place for so long that people get so bored they'll pay ten dollars for a beer.

—Stephen Colbert

**261** When trouble arises and things look bad, there is always one individual who perceives a solution and is willing to take command. Very often, that individual is crazy.

—Dave Barry

**262** One way to tell when you're having an earthquake is your Jell-O stands still.

—Soupy Sales

**263** There's so much pollution in the air now that if it weren't for our lungs, there'd be no place to put it all.

—Robert Orben

**264** I have mixed emotions when I receive my Father's Day gifts. I'm glad my children remember me; I'm disappointed that they think I dress like that.

—Mike Dugan

**265** When Bob Dylan wrote "Hey, Mr. Tambourine Man, play a song for me," did it occur to him that you can't actually play a song on a tambourine?

**266** You know it's time to go on a diet when you're standing next to your car and get a ticket for double-parking.

—Totie Fields

**267** There have been times when I'm stuck on the freeway and I think to myself, "If half the city died right now, I'd be home already."

—Paul Reiser

**268** I do not believe in an afterlife, although I am bringing a change of underwear.

—Woody Allen

**269** I hate the saying "Always a bridesmaid, never a bride." I like to put it into perspective by thinking "Always a pallbearer, never a corpse."

—Laura Kightlinger

**270** Sadly, the bikini that makes you look slimmer has yet to be invented.

—Elizabeth Hurley

**271** My father invented the burglar alarm, which unfortunately was stolen from him.

—Victor Borge

**272** I just bought a Chihuahua. It's the dog for lazy people. You don't have to walk it. Just hold it out the window and squeeze.

—Anthony Clark

**273** Some say "War is not the answer." Depends on the question ... if someone asks "What is raw spelled backwards?," for example.

**274** We spend the first twelve months of our children's lives teaching them to walk and talk, and the next twelve telling them to sit down and shut up.

—Phyllis Diller

**275** Some folks can't handle decision-making very well. Take me, for instance: I have a Ph.D. in Undeclared.

**276** After twelve years of therapy my psychiatrist said something that brought tears to my eyes: "No hablo inglés."

—Ronnie Shakes

**277** The second day of a diet is always easier than the first. By the second you're off it.

—Jackie Gleason

**278** My mother loved children. She would have given anything if I had been one.

—Groucho Marx

**279** In cryogenics they freeze you until science discovers a cure for what killed you, and then they revive you. But what if you froze to death?

—George Miller

**280** I saw a box of macaroni and cheese that said "Cook Thoroughly." Directly underneath were the words "Keep Frozen." I can't do both.

**281** My favorite thing about the Internet is that you get to go into the private world of real creeps without having to smell them.

—Penn Jillette

**282** Happiness is your dentist telling you it won't hurt and then having him catch his hand in the drill.

—Johnny Carson

**283** If I don't eat, I will die. If I'm dead, I can't work. So why aren't my groceries a tax-deductible business expense?

**284** I ... prefer to see the dark side of things. The glass is always half empty. And cracked. And I just cut my lip on it. And chipped a tooth.

—Janeane Garofalo

**285** The universe has come to an end in Houston, where there's a Starbucks across the street from a Starbucks.

—Lewis Black

**286** The scientific theory I like best is that the rings of Saturn are composed entirely of lost airline luggage.

—Mark Russell

**287** When you go into court you are putting your fate into the hands of twelve people who weren't smart enough to get out of jury duty.

—Norm Crosby

**288** Garfield the cat has appeared in the funny papers since the late seventies. As a result, he may be eligible to receive nine Lifetime Achievement Awards.

**289** After silence, that which comes nearest to expressing the inexpressible is music.

—Aldous Huxley

**290** Why do people use the expression "needless to say" before saying something everybody already knew? If you don't need to say it, shut up.

**291** First the doctor told me the good news: I was going to have a disease named after me.

—Steve Martin

**292** I don't own a computer. I'm waiting for the kind where I can look at the screen and say "Hey, I need a pizza" and one comes out and hits me in the eyebrows.

—Kathleen Madigan

**293** It's not really an all-you-can-eat buffet if you can eat things that aren't offered. It's just a some-of-what-you-can-eat buffet.

**294** When I was a kid in elementary school, the teacher asked me to discuss "Moby-Dick." So I said, "It strikes me as a plug for the whaling industry."

—John Astin

**295** The government says only thirty-three percent of Americans have returned their census forms. How do they know that?

—Colin Quinn

**296** They should put expiration dates on clothing so we men will know when they go out of style.

—Garry Shandling

**297** Last night I ordered an entire meal in French, and even the waiter was surprised. It was a Chinese restaurant.

—Henny Youngman

**298** Comedy is when you accidentally fall off a cliff and die. Tragedy is when I have a hangnail.

—Mel Brooks

**299** If variety is the spice of life, marriage is the big can of leftover Spam.

—Johnny Carson

**300** Congratulations—you have just solved cryptogram number three hundred. I have no good reason to mention this.

**301** I got an A in philosophy because I proved that my professor didn't exist.

—Judy Tenuta

**302** Some crossword solvers ask for tips on how to complete a puzzle faster. Simply do what I do—put an I in every square.

**303** The reason grandparents and grandchildren get along so well is that they have a common enemy.

—Sam Levenson

**304** A typical Sunday crossword has about one hundred and forty answers, maybe ten of which comprise the theme. Think about your college days—If you wrote a term paper that was ninety-three percent off-topic, you'd get an F.

**305** I used to compete in sports, and then I realized: You can buy trophies. Now I'm good at everything.

—Demetri Martin

**306** It's amazing that the amount of news that happens in the world every day always just exactly fits the newspaper.

—Jerry Seinfeld

**307** I can tell I'm getting older, because I find myself using words like "spacious," "roomy," and "comfortable" when I'm buying underwear.

—Reno Goodale

**308** I've decided my epitaph will be "He did everything the doctors told him to. Ironic, ain't it?"

**309** In elementary school, in case of fire you have to line up quietly in a single file from smallest to largest. What is the logic? Do tall people burn slower?

—Warren Hutcherson

**310** If it weren't for the fact that the TV set and the refrigerator are so far apart, some of us wouldn't get any exercise at all.

—Joey Adams

**311** Book idea: a huge collection of, say, two thousand of those Japanese number-grid puzzles. Call it "Beaucoup Sudoku."

**312** I do clean up a little. If company is coming, I'll wipe the lipstick off the milk container.

—Elayne Boosler

**313** At first I thought that my life was going around in circles. Then I got to looking closer, and it's actually a downward spiral.

—Tom Ryan

**314** My husband and I didn't sign a prenuptial agreement. We signed a mutual suicide pact.

—Roseanne Barr

**315** I am the product of a mixed marriage. My father was a man and my mother was a woman.

**316** When I was a kid we made money by going to the houses of people who hadn't shoveled their snow, slipping, and suing them.

—Bill Braudis

**317** It is a curious fact that people are never so trivial as when they take themselves seriously.

—Oscar Wilde

**318** In a perfect world, rap music would not have to take the blame for gang activity. Square dance music would.

**319** Sometimes it takes three people to zip me up, but once a dress gets past my hips, it's always worth it.

—Marissa Jaret Winokur

**320** My favorite health club is the International House of Pancakes. Because no matter what you weigh, there will always be someone who weighs a hundred and fifty pounds more than you.

—Lewis Black

**321** Human beings are the only creatures that allow their children to come back home.

—Bill Cosby

**322** If I'm ever stuck on a respirator or a life-support system, I definitely want to be unplugged. But not until I'm down to a size eight.

—Henriette Mantel

**323** Thanksgiving is an emotional time. People travel thousands of miles to be with people they only see once a year, and then discover once a year is way too often.

—Johnny Carson

**324** I gave my cat a bath the other day.... He enjoyed it, it was fun for me. The fur would stick to my tongue, but other than that ...

—Steve Martin

**325** I will never forget my first day of school. My mom woke me up, got me dressed, made my bed, and fed me. Man, did the guys in the dorm tease me.

—Michael Aronin

**326** The bartender asked me, "What'll you have?" I said "Surprise me." He showed me a naked picture of my wife.

—Rodney Dangerfield

**327** When the weather report says there's a flash flood warning in effect until noon, I always wonder how the water knows what time to stop.

**328** On cable TV they have a Weather Channel, twenty-four hours of weather. We had something like that where I grew up. We called it a window.

—Dan Spencer

**329** Outside of a dog, a book is man's best friend. Inside of a dog, it's too dark to read.

—Groucho Marx

**330** I grew up with six brothers. That's how I learned to dance ... waiting for the bathroom.

—Bob Hope

**331** They say, "Guns don't kill people, people kill people." But I think the guns help. Just standing there saying "Bang!" doesn't really hurt anybody.

—Eddie Izzard

**332** You can learn a lot from the Discovery Channel. For example, the world's largest human breasts, unenhanced by surgery, were size forty-eight-V.

**333** My kindergarten teacher hated me. She used to find any excuse to pick on me, especially during nap time. Like I'm the only guy who sleeps naked.

—Brian Kiley

**334** A suicide hotline is where they talk to you until you don't feel like killing yourself. Exactly the opposite of telemarketing.

—Dana Snow

**335** Human beings are seventy percent water, and with some, the rest is collagen.

—Martin Mull

**336** Found on Twitter: I attribute most of my good days to a couple of people with voodoo dolls canceling each other out.

**337** Crosswords use words that we could but don't. Have you ever looked at your watch and said, "My gosh, look at the time! I have to hie!"?

**338** I was so self-conscious that when I was at a football game and the players went into a huddle, I thought they were talking about me.

—Jackie Mason

**339** Women complain that men don't do enough, but it's your own fault. You train your man to do nothing. You can't blame someone for not knowing what his or her job should be.

—Jennifer Aniston

**340** You know what bugs me? People who smoke cigars in restaurants. That's why I always carry a water pistol filled with gasoline.

—Paul Provenza

**341** My parents didn't love me. They bronzed my baby shoes with my feet still in them.

—Woody Allen

**342** Last Christmas ... I gave my kid a BB gun. He gave me a sweatshirt with a bull's-eye on the back.

—Rodney Dangerfield

**343** One year I played Little League baseball and my dad was the coach. Halfway through the season he traded me to another family.

—David Corrado

**344** I find low self-esteem incomprehensible. Why hate yourself, when you can hate others?

—Amy Ashton

**345** I've thought about having a family. I just haven't seen any that really appeal to me.

—Laura Kightlinger

**346** The pen is mightier than the sword and considerably easier to write with.

—Marty Feldman

**347** Assuming that either the left wing or the right wing gained control of the country, it would probably fly around in circles.

—Pat Paulsen

**348** I don't have pet peeves like some people. I have whole kennels of irritation.

—Whoopi Goldberg

**349** The uses of tobacco aren't obvious right off the bat. You shred it up, put it on a piece of paper, roll it up and stick it between your lips ... and set fire to it.

—Bob Newhart

**350** Of course we need firearms. You never know when some nut is going to come up to you and say something like, "You're fired." You gotta be ready.

—Dave Attell

**351** If alcohol is flammable, why don't people who drink and smoke just burst into flames?

**352** A Croatian man returned a book to his local library forty years after borrowing it, during which time he never got around to reading it.

**353** When I was about ten we moved because my father sold our house. Somehow the landlord found out about it, and we had to go.

—A. Whitney Brown

**354** ESPN and Court TV together let me follow the careers of all my favorite athletes.

—Jeff Stilson

**355** If the eyes are the windows to the soul, then why does it hurt when I spray them with Windex?

—Stephen Colbert

**356** According to modern astronomers, space is finite. This is a very comforting thought, particularly for people who cannot remember where they left things.

—Woody Allen

**357** The only thing to do with family skeletons is to take them out of the closet and dance with them.

—Author unknown

**358** I have property in Los Angeles. A hotel is holding two of my suitcases.

—Soupy Sales

**359** If I bought a sudoku book, it would mean the terrorists have won.

—American Crossword
Puzzle Tournament
regular Ellen Ripstein

**360** Congratulations ... if you found the secret message hidden in these cryptograms, you might be a conspiracy theorist.

# FIRST HINTS

| | | | | | |
|---|---|---|---|---|---|
| 1 Q→H | 61 D→N | 121 C→M | 181 U→G | 241 R→B | 301 B→O |
| 2 S→L | 62 C→O | 122 V→L | 182 J→V | 242 T→Y | 302 F→P |
| 3 V→L | 63 F→C | 123 F→S | 183 M→W | 243 G→W | 303 V→E |
| 4 W→A | 64 R→I | 124 R→W | 184 I→L | 244 N→L | 304 G→O |
| 5 E→R | 65 T→N | 125 H→G | 185 O→A | 245 H→I | 305 H→A |
| 6 D→A | 66 N→R | 126 N→G | 186 P→R | 246 U→B | 306 M→U |
| 7 C→M | 67 H→W | 127 Y→N | 187 A→M | 247 J→G | 307 I→T |
| 8 F→V | 68 Z→T | 128 W→P | 188 B→X | 248 M→P | 308 L→Y |
| 9 R→H | 69 J→S | 129 U→L | 189 X→O | 249 K→L | 309 P→A |
| 10 T→W | 70 M→S | 130 M→U | 190 S→H | 250 L→O | 310 Q→J |
| 11 G→B | 71 I→W | 131 O→I | 191 E→T | 251 V→D | 311 A→D |
| 12 B→R | 72 Z→C | 132 L→M | 192 V→B | 252 Q→R | 312 Z→A |
| 13 N→D | 73 O→N | 133 P→G | 193 C→I | 253 Z→S | 313 X→D |
| 14 Q→O | 74 P→N | 134 Q→N | 194 V→A | 254 X→W | 314 S→Y |
| 15 Y→P | 75 H→U | 135 A→R | 195 F→R | 255 W→U | 315 W→N |
| 16 O→T | 76 Q→O | 136 Z→L | 196 K→S | 256 E→S | 316 D→A |
| 17 J→S | 77 A→F | 137 X→B | 197 R→S | 257 D→K | 317 V→N |
| 18 K→Y | 78 S→B | 138 S→F | 198 T→C | 258 V→N | 318 W→S |
| 19 O→D | 79 W→A | 139 E→V | 199 G→C | 259 F→Y | 319 F→Z |
| 20 L→Y | 80 E→L | 140 D→I | 200 H→T | 260 G→A | 320 R→P |
| 21 B→F | 81 D→U | 141 C→E | 201 U→A | 261 B→N | 321 S→W |
| 22 P→H | 82 C→D | 142 F→G | 202 B→T | 262 H→A | 322 T→M |
| 23 A→O | 83 F→H | 143 R→H | 203 K→M | 263 U→N | 323 G→T |
| 24 N→E | 84 G→W | 144 T→F | 204 I→E | 264 M→E | 324 B→W |
| 25 X→S | 85 B→P | 145 G→H | 205 O→Y | 265 M→Y | 325 H→C |
| 26 T→I | 86 Y→R | 146 L→U | 206 P→F | 266 I→Y | 326 J→K |
| 27 S→W | 87 U→F | 147 N→A | 207 Q→T | 267 L→M | 327 K→C |
| 28 T→G | 88 M→A | 148 Y→L | 208 A→L | 268 P→E | 328 L→U |
| 29 W→N | 89 K→S | 149 U→I | 209 E→L | 269 Q→O | 329 P→I |
| 30 E→A | 90 O→M | 150 M→K | 210 Z→M | 270 A→V | 330 Q→R |
| 31 C→P | 91 O→H | 151 Q→F | 211 X→A | 271 Z→V | 331 A→I |
| 32 V→M | 92 Q→C | 152 A→H | 212 D→Y | 272 X→O | 332 Z→L |
| 33 B→D | 93 A→B | 153 Z→E | 213 D→N | 273 W→I | 333 X→M |
| 34 R→X | 94 Z→A | 154 X→V | 214 Q→A | 274 E→G | 334 F→X |
| 35 G→Z | 95 S→I | 155 S→V | 215 R→I | 275 D→U | 335 E→U |
| 36 N→U | 96 E→X | 156 W→S | 216 T→W | 276 C→H | 336 V→T |
| 37 Y→W | 97 H→L | 157 D→V | 217 G→R | 277 V→O | 337 R→M |
| 38 A→T | 98 D→F | 158 U→D | 218 B→Y | 278 F→R | 338 T→F |
| 39 U→Y | 99 C→P | 159 J→S | 219 N→H | 279 R→O | 339 W→Y |
| 40 M→N | 100 E→C | 160 V→O | 220 H→I | 280 T→I | 340 G→T |
| 41 K→W | 101 F→N | 161 F→U | 221 Y→F | 281 G→I | 341 B→D |
| 42 I→W | 102 R→J | 162 R→Y | 222 U→W | 282 N→G | 342 N→W |
| 43 O→L | 103 G→T | 163 T→O | 223 J→Y | 283 H→W | 343 H→C |
| 44 L→H | 104 B→Y | 164 B→Y | 224 M→G | 284 Y→F | 344 Y→N |
| 45 Z→W | 105 N→T | 165 N→I | 225 K→I | 285 J→A | 345 U→Y |
| 46 S→O | 106 Y→H | 166 M→A | 226 I→L | 286 M→G | 346 J→R |
| 47 W→D | 107 U→F | 167 K→E | 227 O→S | 287 K→A | 347 M→O |
| 48 D→C | 108 J→R | 168 O→L | 228 S→W | 288 I→E | 348 K→M |
| 49 N→E | 109 M→O | 169 V→G | 229 L→I | 289 O→R | 349 I→C |
| 50 Y→R | 110 I→G | 170 P→F | 230 P→L | 290 P→B | 350 L→U |
| 51 U→V | 111 O→L | 171 E→T | 231 Q→I | 291 A→M | 351 P→N |
| 52 J→X | 112 L→S | 172 W→R | 232 A→I | 292 Z→N | 352 Q→D |
| 53 I→Y | 113 P→V | 173 D→O | 233 Z→U | 293 X→G | 353 S→I |
| 54 O→G | 114 Q→D | 174 C→R | 234 C→S | 294 Y→J | 354 E→D |
| 55 L→J | 115 A→W | 175 R→V | 235 X→O | 295 S→L | 355 D→W |
| 56 P→S | 116 Z→B | 176 T→W | 236 W→V | 296 W→G | 356 V→G |
| 57 Q→I | 117 X→L | 177 G→E | 237 E→V | 297 E→H | 357 T→I |
| 58 A→R | 118 S→C | 178 N→I | 238 D→E | 298 D→S | 358 G→P |
| 59 Z→A | 119 E→N | 179 H→O | 239 V→K | 299 U→S | 359 N→A |
| 60 W→D | 120 D→B | 180 Y→I | 240 F→V | 300 T→V | 360 Y→G |

# SECOND HINTS

| | | | | | |
|---|---|---|---|---|---|
| 1 U→P | 61 G→H | 121 O→C | 181 X→U | 241 E→L | 301 E→P |
| 2 J→G | 62 B→H | 122 P→E | 182 S→P | 242 V→N | 302 Z→C |
| 3 L→V | 63 H→U | 123 Z→L | 183 W→M | 243 F→V | 303 A→M |
| 4 M→R | 64 U→L | 124 A→G | 184 D→Y | 244 R→B | 304 W→U |
| 5 K→H | 65 J→W | 125 Z→S | 185 C→Y | 245 T→E | 305 D→P |
| 6 I→V | 66 M→P | 126 X→H | 186 R→H | 246 B→L | 306 F→W |
| 7 O→G | 67 K→M | 127 S→I | 187 T→D | 247 N→Y | 307 R→O |
| 8 P→K | 68 T→S | 128 B→S | 188 Q→H | 248 H→I | 308 B→O |
| 9 Q→F | 69 L→G | 129 E→O | 189 G→C | 249 U→S | 309 B→O |
| 10 A→V | 70 P→L | 130 D→O | 190 B→A | 250 J→C | 310 N→W |
| 11 Z→K | 71 Q→Y | 131 C→P | 191 N→M | 251 L→O | 311 H→R |
| 12 X→H | 72 W→M | 132 V→S | 192 H→N | 252 I→T | 312 Y→D |
| 13 S→O | 73 A→I | 133 F→H | 193 Y→H | 253 O→J | 313 U→T |
| 14 W→G | 74 Z→T | 134 R→S | 194 M→E | 254 Q→G | 314 J→E |
| 15 E→K | 75 X→G | 135 N→U | 195 I→N | 255 A→R | 315 M→O |
| 16 D→I | 76 X→N | 136 J→E | 196 E→W | 256 Z→T | 316 K→U |
| 17 V→J | 77 S→M | 137 M→N | 197 O→T | 257 X→O | 317 O→Y |
| 18 R→H | 78 E→H | 138 K→N | 198 L→T | 258 S→C | 318 J→I |
| 19 T→A | 79 D→H | 139 L→G | 199 P→O | 259 W→U | 319 L→E |
| 20 Z→O | 80 C→D | 140 P→R | 200 X→Y | 260 E→S | 320 Q→Y |
| 21 X→L | 81 V→M | 141 Q→T | 201 W→G | 261 D→G | 321 U→S |
| 22 B→C | 82 F→U | 142 A→R | 202 K→E | 262 C→J | 322 Z→O |
| 23 N→V | 83 R→T | 143 X→E | 203 D→K | 263 F→R | 323 X→Y |
| 24 Y→U | 84 B→N | 144 S→P | 204 C→N | 264 R→S | 324 S→U |
| 25 U→M | 85 Z→Y | 145 W→V | 205 V→D | 265 T→U | 325 W→D |
| 26 A→S | 86 S→N | 146 T→G | 206 R→S | 266 G→I | 326 E→G |
| 27 M→O | 87 W→A | 147 E→P | 207 T→W | 267 N→Y | 327 D→R |
| 28 Q→B | 88 D→N | 148 C→T | 208 B→S | 268 H→V | 328 C→I |
| 29 I→K | 89 V→C | 149 V→O | 209 M→H | 269 Y→C | 329 V→K |
| 30 O→F | 90 F→P | 150 F→W | 210 Y→H | 270 J→E | 330 T→L |
| 31 L→D | 91 T→N | 151 B→O | 211 U→I | 271 M→S | 331 B→P |
| 32 P→D | 92 N→A | 152 N→D | 212 K→L | 272 K→D | 332 N→E |
| 33 M→A | 93 H→D | 153 H→W | 213 I→O | 273 I→A | 333 Y→S |
| 34 Q→R | 94 Y→T | 154 U→F | 214 A→H | 274 P→E | 334 L→W |
| 35 Z→F | 95 J→G | 155 J→O | 215 L→C | 275 A→S | 335 M→W |
| 36 W→E | 96 V→E | 156 I→L | 216 P→Y | 276 Z→E | 336 O→E |
| 37 D→G | 97 W→T | 157 P→H | 217 A→M | 277 X→H | 337 P→O |
| 38 K→M | 98 K→M | 158 E→M | 218 Z→U | 278 S→O | 338 Q→C |
| 39 V→C | 99 I→Y | 159 D→O | 219 X→B | 279 W→A | 339 J→E |
| 40 R→F | 100 Q→P | 160 Q→N | 220 S→U | 280 E→S | 340 Y→P |
| 41 G→C | 101 L→H | 161 A→W | 221 D→E | 281 D→U | 341 Z→L |
| 42 H→L | 102 Q→S | 162 Z→H | 222 C→M | 282 C→L | 342 S→M |
| 43 Y→S | 103 Z→I | 163 X→C | 223 F→K | 283 V→E | 343 W→M |
| 44 U→A | 104 X→D | 164 S→B | 224 R→C | 284 F→D | 344 E→H |
| 45 B→N | 105 S→C | 165 W→T | 225 T→C | 285 T→K | 345 C→N |
| 46 O→C | 106 E→L | 166 C→Y | 226 G→N | 286 G→U | 346 V→A |
| 47 L→I | 107 D→S | 167 V→S | 227 B→R | 287 B→V | 347 R→C |
| 48 P→B | 108 C→F | 168 F→P | 228 I→L | 288 N→C | 348 B→G |
| 49 A→H | 109 G→R | 169 U→P | 229 N→O | 289 H→L | 349 N→D |
| 50 Z→U | 110 F→R | 170 R→A | 230 H→T | 290 U→I | 350 G→E |
| 51 X→O | 111 R→S | 171 T→W | 231 Y→E | 291 J→S | 351 H→L |
| 52 S→O | 112 T→B | 172 B→S | 232 U→A | 292 M→W | 352 Y→E |
| 53 W→O | 113 B→I | 173 H→T | 233 M→C | 293 K→R | 353 U→M |
| 54 E→T | 114 H→J | 174 Y→F | 234 B→L | 294 C→W | 354 D→F |
| 55 D→H | 115 Y→N | 175 M→H | 235 J→S | 295 O→S | 355 K→R |
| 56 C→R | 116 U→A | 176 K→M | 236 O→N | 296 L→O | 356 I→H |
| 57 V→D | 117 J→W | 177 O→L | 237 L→N | 297 P→V | 357 L→A |
| 58 F→V | 118 M→T | 178 L→H | 238 A→P | 298 Q→E | 358 Q→Y |
| 59 R→G | 119 K→Y | 179 Q→S | 239 S→R | 299 V→R | 359 A→R |
| 60 T→N | 120 I→D | 180 A→U | 240 W→P | 300 S→J | 360 Z→C |